101st Airborne in Normandy

101st Airborne in Normandy

A History in Period Photographs

Dominique François

Schiffer Military History
Atglen, PA

Dedication

This book is dedicated to my wife Gaélle,
and to my children
Aurélien, Corentin, and Eilean.

Acknowledgments

The author is deeply indebted to a number of individuals who provided great assistance in the completition of this project.

Z. Frank Hanner, Director of the National Infantry Museum, Fort Benning, Georgia, who was very helpful in providing photographs from Fort Benning. Bernard Foucher, who was very generous in making available photographs of his personal collection for use in this book. And Mrs. Anita Colomb, who was very helpful in translating the manuscript.

Finally, this book could never have been completed without the assistance of my wife, Gaëlle François, who as an advisor is unsurpassed.

Book Design by Ian Robertson.

Library of Congress Control Number: 2005934652

Printed in China.
ISBN: 0-7643-2424-1

We are interested in hearing from authors with book ideas on related topics.

Published by Schiffer Publishing Ltd.
4880 Lower Valley Road
Atglen, PA 19310
Phone: (610) 593-1777
FAX: (610) 593-2002
E-mail: Info@schifferbooks.com.
Visit our web site at: www.schifferbooks.com
Please write for a free catalog.
This book may be purchased from the publisher.
Please include $3.95 postage.
Try your bookstore first.

In Europe, Schiffer books are distributed by:
Bushwood Books
6 Marksbury Avenue
Kew Gardens
Surrey TW9 4JF
England
Phone: 44 (0) 20 8392-8585
FAX: 44 (0) 20 8392-9876
E-mail: Info@bushwoodbooks.co.uk.
Free postage in the UK. Europe: air mail at cost.
Try your bookstore first.

Contents

1

Reactivation and Training

After the activation of the 101st Airborne Division on 16 August 1942 at Camp Claiborne, Louisiana, Major General William C. Lee observed that, "The 101st...has no history, but it has a rendezvous with destiny." Time and time again, the 101st has kept that rendezvous and, in so doing, has acquired a proud history.

The 101st Airborne Division traces its lineage to World War I with the formation of the 101st Division on 23 July 1918. It was demobilized on 11 December 1918 as a result of the armistice. In 1921, the 101st Infantry Division reconstitued and reorganized as a reserve unit, with its headquarters in Milwaukee, Wisconsin.

On 15 August 1942 the division disbanded as a reserve unit, and was activated in the United States Army as the 101st Airborne Division.

Following the suggestion of Major William C. Lee, the War Department formed the first parachute unit—a test platoon—at Fort Benning, Georgia. This platoon, consisting of volunteers from the 29th Infantry Regiment, made its first jump on 16 August 1940. The success of this unit led to the establishment of several parachute battalions and regiments during the following two years.

In 1942 Major Lee, by now brigadier general, endorsed the concept of airborne divisions after studying the British Army's use of parachute troops during the early years of World War II. The commander of Army ground forces, Lieutenant General Lesley J. McNair, concurred with Lee's recommendations, and ordered the formation of the 82nd and the 101st Airborne Divisions. The initial personnel and equipment for both divisions came from the 82nd Motorized Infantry Division, which inactivated at the same time. Brigadier General Lee assumed command of the 101st Airborne Division on 19 August 1942.

Originally, the 101st had one parachute regiment (the 402nd Parachute Infantry), two glider regiments (the 327th and the 401st Glider Infantries), and three artillery battalions (the 377th Parachute Field Artillery, 321st Glider Field Artillery, and the 907th Glider Field Artillery). Additional support units were the 326th Airborne Medical Company and the 426th Airborne Quartermaster Company.

Organizing and training the new division was a challenge. In October, the 101st began rigourous training at Fort Bragg. Throughout the fall and winter, General Lee helped to establish a whole new tactic of warfare—the use of airborne troops in battle.

In June 1943 the 101st received a second parachute regiment, the 506th Parachute Infantry from Camp Toccoa, Georgia. The 506th had trained in the shadow of Currahee Mountain, and had adopted the name "Currahee" as its motto. That summer the division proved itself during the "Tenessee Maneuver," and the Army deployed it to England.

Young Abe

The American Eagle mascot of the 101st was the flesh-and-blood counterpart of the division's "Screaming Eagle" shoulder patch. Although the 101st was the first of its kind in military history, Young Abe was not. Abe was said to be a direct descendant of a famous Civil War mascot named "Old Abe," who survived 28 battles with the 8th Wisconsin Regiment. According to history, Old Abe would go into a fight perched between the regimental colors and the American flag. During the action, Old Abe would fly screaming from his perch and flap his wings excitedly from the end of his leash, as though he were urging the troops on to victory. Unfortunately, Young Abe never saw action with his outfit. He died at Fort Bragg while the division was in Tenessee.

The 101st Airborne Division boarded ships in New York Harbor, and arrived in England 10 days later. They spent 10 months in the counties of Bershire and Wiltshire, training six days a week. Units worked in close combat, night operations, street fighting, combat field exercises, chemical warfare, and a number of other military subjects, in addition to demanding physical training, which included hikes of 25 miles. They also trained in the use of German weapons. In October, the 101st began its own jump school to train over 400 new personnel and key members of non-jump units of the 101st.

In January 1944 the newly nicknamed Eagle Division received a third parachute regiment, the 501st Parachute Infantry. Two months later, the 401st Glider Infantry Regiment detached one battalion to be a part of the 82nd Airborne Division.

Major General Lee suffered a heart attack in February and returned to the United States. Major General Maxwell D. Taylor became the new commander.

Meanwhile, the Supreme Headquarters Allied Expeditionary Force planned an invasion of Northern France, and called it Operation OVERLORD. The mission of the 101st was to jump in before the waterborne invasion forces landed on the beach. The paratroopers would secure exits from the beachhead, and prevent these areas from receiving German reinforcements.

In preparation for its mission, the 101st participated in three Army-wide exercises: BEAVER, TIGER, and EAGLE. In May, elements of the division began leaving their training areas for the airfields and marshalling areas. They would not assemble again until they met on the drop zones of France.

At 15 minutes after midnight on 6 June 1944, Captain Frank L. Lillyman led his team of the 101st Pathfinders out the door of a C-47 aircraft, and landed in occupied France. Behind the Pathfinders came 6,000 paratroopers of the 101st Airborne Division in C-47s of the IX Troop Carrier Command. D-Day began. Running into heavy German flak as they approached the drop zones, many of the troop aircraft took evasive action and scattered the jumpers over a wide area. By nightfall, only 2,500 men could re-assemble in their units....

In March 1944, paratroopers of the 377th Parachute Field Artillery Battalion of the 101st Airborne assemble a 75mm canon Howitzer during a "Beaver" drill in England. (NARA)

The 75mm canon Howitzer may be airdropped in seven containers. (NARA)

23 March, 1944: Winston Churchill, General Dwight Eisenhower, and General Maxwell Taylor attend maneuvers of the 101st Airborne in England. (NARA)

23 March, 1944, an airdrop of divisional scale is carried out during the drill. (NARA)

Prime Minister Winston Churchill handles the weapons used by the U.S. paratroopers, here a Bazooka. (NARA)

Lt. Louis Schadagg of the Airborne Medical Corps and the Secretary of State, Edward Stettinius, 20 April, 1944. (NARA)

On April 12, 1944, General Eisenhower meets with English paratroopers. Like their American comrades, they will have to jump behind enemy lines. (NARA)

General Eisenhower and Lieutenant Colonet Eric Yeldman of the Corps of English paratroopers. (NARA)

Parachute ration: the paratroopers only packed sufficient food for 48 hours during Operation Neptune. (NARA)

Fort Bragg, 1943: A practice jump from a C-47. This interesting photograph features three types of parachutes. (NARA)

These artillery men of an airborne artillery battalion set up a 75mm Howitzer canon. (NARA)

101st Airborne Division patch "Screaming Eagles." (Coll. D. François)

"Young Abe": The American mascot of the 101st Airborne Division. (NARA)

A C-47 flies over a mountainous region of the U.S. during jump training. (NARA)

These gliders are being taken out of Waco factories in Troy, Ohio and will soon be on their way to different operation sights. (NARA)

Fort Benning: Facilities where parachutes are folded. (NARA)

1941: Two paratroopers of the 501st Parachute Battalion take part in a drill at Fort Benning. (NARA)

The 250-foot tower at Fort Benning was used to train parachute troops. (Fort Benning National Infantry Museum)

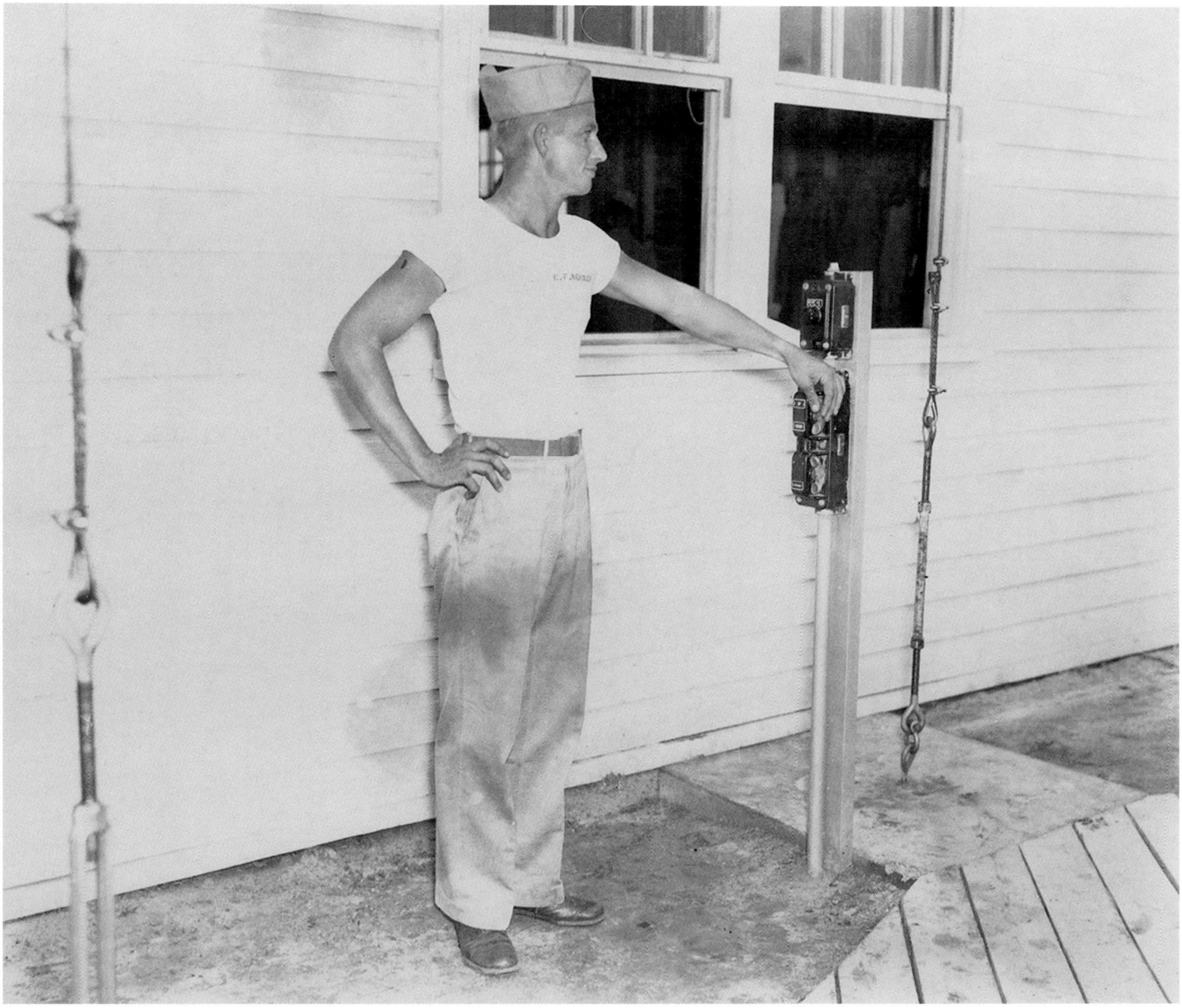

Command post: the 250-foot tower.

The base of the 250-foot tower.

Two of the 250-foot towers at Fort Benning.

Demonstration from the 250-foot tower.

Base of the 250-foot tower.

Fort Benning: One of the obstacle courses designed for paratroopers.

The safe arrival of a paratrooper in Fort Benning.

Top: Rough landing of a DZ at Fort Benning. Bottom: Members of the Parachute Test Platoon during an early practice jump. Practice jumps began during the eigth week of training.

Above: Recovery of parachutes on "Frying Pan Drop Zone" at Fort Benning. Below: In the background, Fort Benning: dropping down from the 250-foot tower.

This paratrooper seems to be pleased with his jump. Could it be thanks to his horseshoe?

These young paratroopers receive chocolate bars during a transfer by train.

Parachuting at Fort Benning.

The base of the 250-foot tower.

Training to land.

Training to manipulate the harness.

Training session for the different phases of the jump.

Lighting of the jump sights.

Jumping from one of the 250-foot towers.

Stowing a mountain canon in a C-47.

Above: Stowing a jeep in a C-47. Below: The cabin of a C-47 used for training.

Above: An instructor demonstrates procedures to follow after landing. Below: Ceremony in Columbus: General Lee is facing the officers of the 501st Parachute Battalion. These officers will become the commanders of the various airborne regiments of the U.S. Army.

View of the door.

The national colors are presented to General Lee.

General Lee is in front of the officers of the 501st during a ceremony in Columbus, Georgia. General Lee will later be known as the Father of the U.S. Airborne troops.

Above: A group of officers from Fort Benning. Below: In a few months, General Lee will assume the command of the 101st Airborne Division.

Practice jump at Fort Benning.

Army camps of the 501st Parachute Battalion.

General Lee inspects the men of the 501st parachute Battalion. They will become the ranking officers of future airborne troops.

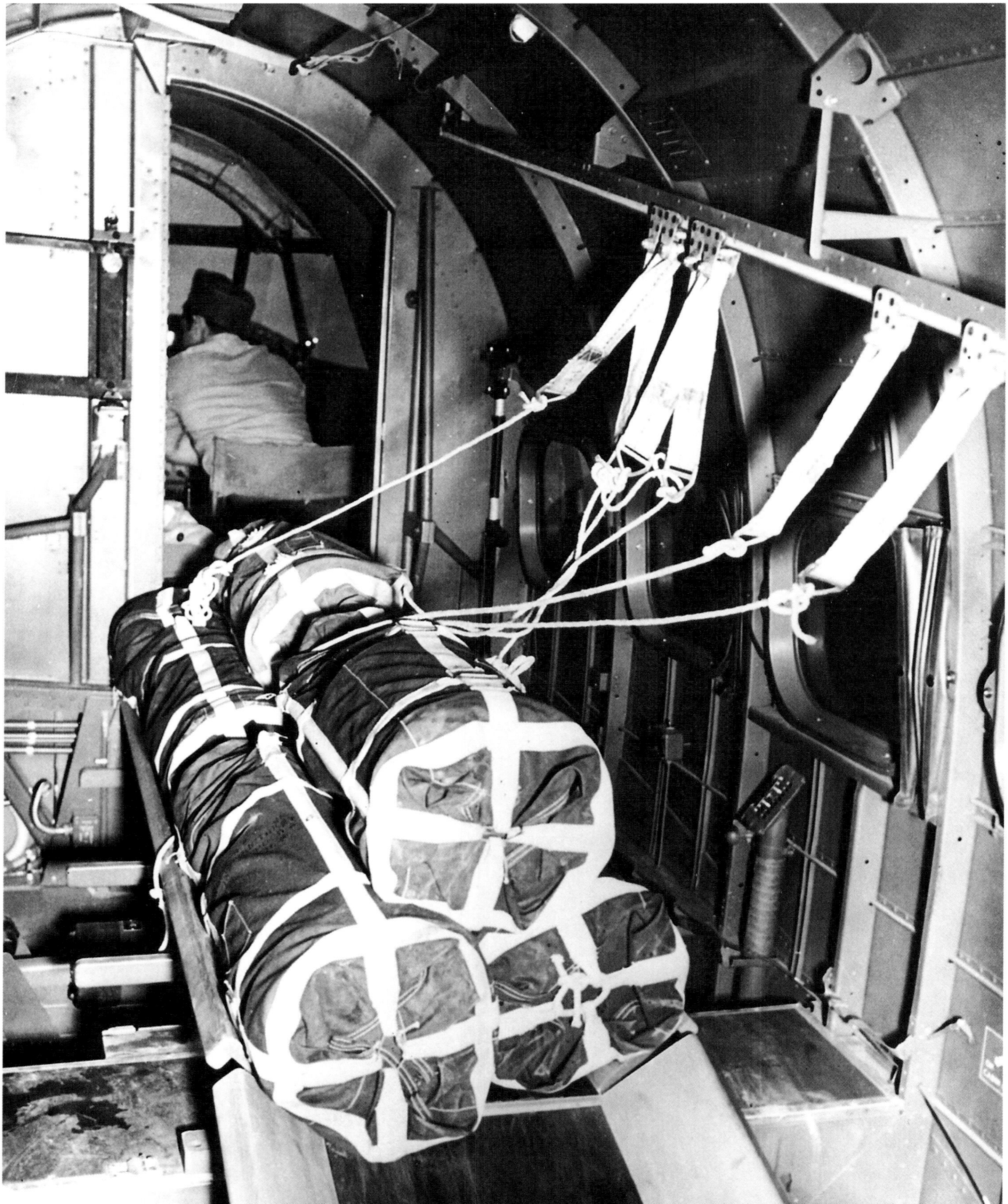

A-5 container drops.

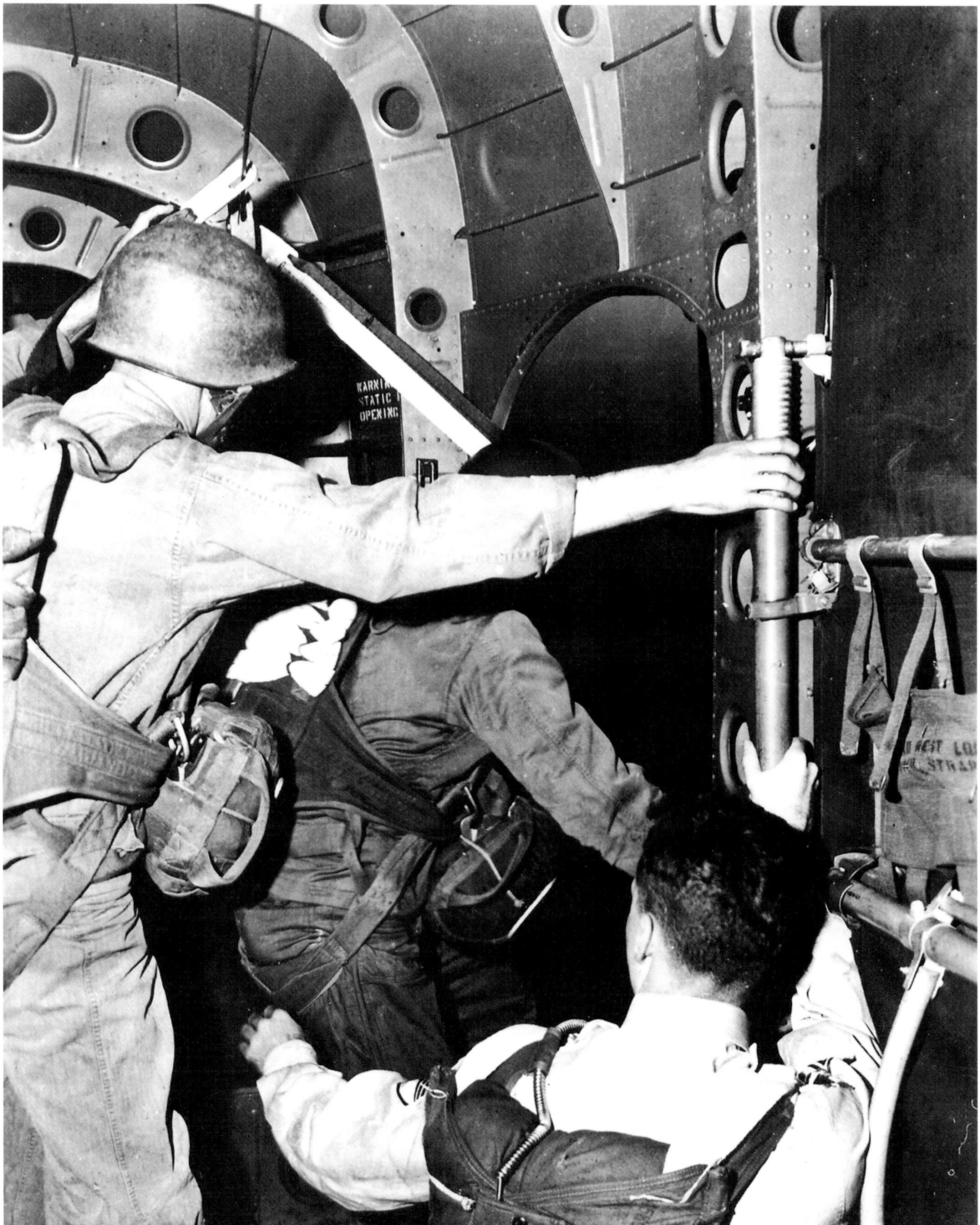

The Jumpmaster gives the departure signal to these two paratroopers. He is equipped with only a back parachute with a manual release.

Two paratroopers wearing the M.1941, the first jumping outfit.

Infiltration training for this paratrooper of the 502nd Parachute Batta ion.

The "Riggers" are responsible for the upkeep of the parachutes.

Training for landing.

Young volunteers of the 506th PIR.

This parachutist demonstrates the position when standing at the doorway of the plane. He is equipped with a T-5 parachute.

Fort Benning: Training to jump from a C-47.

Paratroopers have set up a campsite in the area of Camp Toccoa, GA. (D. François)

A group of young recruits take a few minutes to relax. (D. François)

These paratroopers have just received their "Wings" a few days ago. (D.François)

A campsite in Camp Toccoa.

Brigadier General Anthony C. Mc. Auliffe, Division Artillery Commander. (NARA)

Clockwise from above left: Brigadier General Gerald. J. Higgins, Assistant Commanding General; Brigadier General William N. Gillmore (both NARA); and Colonel Robert Sink, 506th Parachute Infantry Regiment. (506th PIR yearbook)

Brigadier General Mc Auliffe and Brigadier General Higgins. (NARA)

General Maxwell Taylor, Commanding General 101st Airborne Division (NARA)

Major General W. Lee.

Above: Brigadier General Don F. Pratt, Assistant Commanding General of the 101st Airborne Division from activation until 6 June 1944. He was killed in his glider crash at Hiesville on D-Day. Above right: Colonel Chase, 506th PIR, Regimental Executive Officer. Right: Lt. Colonel William T. Turner, 506th PIR.

Above: Lt. Colonel James L. Laprade, 506th PIR.

Left: Lt. Colonel Robert L. Strayer, 506th PIR.

Lt. Colonel Robert Wolwerton, 506th PIR.

Captain Richard Winters, Commanding Officer Easy Company, 506th PIR.

Training in England, a few weeks before the Landings. (NARA)

2

Organic Units

501st Parachute Infantry Regiment

Commanding the 501st Parachute Infantry was the U.S. Army's most flamboyant parachute officer: Colonel Howard R. Johnson. Originally Johnson had started out his military career as a sailor. But after two years as a midshipman at Annapolis he transferred to the Army, and became an infantry officer. Much like the Armored Corps' General George S. Patton, Johnson had no patience for weakness of any kind among his subordinates, and he seemed to have an insatiable desire to prove how tough and brave he was. Shortly after forming his regiment at Camp Toccoa, Georgia, Johnson took it to Fort Benning for jump training. And while his troops were learning the basics of parachuting, Johnson, already a qualified paratrooper, would demonstrate the kind of courage he expected from everyone by personnally making, depending on the weather, three to five five jumps a day. He frequently yelled at his assembled regiment "We are the best!" the fire-eating Johnson promised to lead the 501st into battle and win the war with it. And when the war was over the 501st had as good a claim on winning it as any fighting outfit did. But Colonel Johnson never lived to boast about the feats of his beloved regiment. Carrying into battle his overpowering urge to constantly display his fearlessness, the Colonel would always refuse to take cover while under German artillery fire. His bravery was to cost him his life in Holland and deprive America of one of its finest combat leaders.

Colonel Howard Johnson, 501st Parachute Infantry Regiment. (NARA)

LTC Julian J. Ewell, who succeeded Colonel Johnson as CO of the 501st. (NARA)

501st PIR patch. (coll. D. François)

502nd Parachute Infantry Regiment

In July of 1941 the 502nd Parachute Battalion was formed. The 502's history would begin with a bang when they jumped twice in Carolina maneuvers that year. The expansion of the U.S. Army Airborne program continued to grow, and on January 30, 1942, the 502nd expanded from a battalion to a regiment.

On March 2, 1942, the 502nd Parachute Infantry was activated under the command of Lt. Col. George P. Howell. When the unit was formed it had much of the same personnel as it had when it was activated as a battalion back in 1941. It should also be noted that the 502nd was the only parachute regiment that maintained its identity and personnel from its inception as a battalion. Shortly after the formation of the unit Col. Howell left to take command of the Parachute school at Fort Bragg. Command was handed over to his executive officer, Lt.Col. George Van Horn Moseley, a West Pointer who quickly began to form the regiment into his own liking. His rigorous work effort and will power, which he instilled on his men, would go a long way in forming their future combat record.

The 502nd would become the original parachute infantry regiment of the 101st Division. Shortly after they became part of the 101st, they moved from Fort Benning to join the rest of the division, which was stationed at Fort Bragg.

Throughout the rest of 1942 and into 1943, the 502nd PIR took part in a grueling training program, which consisted of individual, unit, and combined division training. During March 1942 they took part in division maneuvers in Southern Pines. This was followed by the Camden maneuvers, which started on May 23rd of that year. Shortly after the Camden Maneuvers, the big Tenessee maneuvers were held. It was during the Tenessee Maneuvers that we would get a glimpse of what the 502nd was made of when men of H Company set a new marching record. They marched a total of 145.5 miles in 57.25 hours, in which the first 33 miles were done in 11 hours.

On September 4th, 1943, men of the 502nd boarded the *SS. Strathnaver*, bound for their new home in England. The *Strathnaver* sailed for 6 days before she had to make port on September 11 in St. Johns, Newfoundland, for repairs. It was discovered that the ship's fresh water tanks had salt water in them. The 502nd was in port from September 11th to the 26th. During this time in St. Johns the men did not get to rest. They took part in road marches, barrack inspections drills, and physical conditioning exercises. On September 26th the ship headed back out to sea, only to return again after striking some rocks in the harbor. On the 27th she made another attempt to leave, but returned to port after taking on some 28 inches of water. Here the men stayed stranded, continuing the routine until October 4th, when *SS John Ericsson* picked the men up and set sail for England. On October 18th the ship finally arrived in Liverpool. The journey would end up taking a total of 44 days.

When the deuce arrived in England they boarded military trucks, and headed for what would be their home for the next 7 months. They settled into quarters in Chilton Foliat and Denford, near Hungerford, Berkshire. The first days and weeks were spent getting used to their new surroundings. The quaint countryside surroundings, in which they would be living, were a far cry from their days at Fort Bragg.

The deuce men could not ponder their setting for long, because their days were soon filled with physical condition training that would include 15-25 mile hikes and daily close combat exercises. Instructions were given in a wide variety of items from First aid, map reading, chemical warfare, and the use and firing of German weapons. Company and battalion size parachute drops where also practiced during this period.

During the winter a couple things took place which would affect the deuce. Captain Frank Lillyman, Commander of I-Company, departed for a new assignment as the commander of the 101st pathfinders. Lillyman was replaced by Captain Ivan Hershner, who commanded the unit until June 9, 1944. The 502nd was also given its call sign, or unit code (kickoff), which it would retain throughout the war.

In early spring, the soldiers of the deuce participated in a number of full-scale exercises. In March it was Exercise Beaver, in April Exercise Tiger, and in May Exercise Eagle, which would

502nd PIR patch. (Coll. D. François)

be the deuce's dress rehearsal for the D-Day Invasion of Fortress Europe. Each time the men rehearsed capturing key bridges leading inland from the shore, and the destruction of mock gun positions. It was during Exercise Eagle that ominous misfortune arrived. Eight of the nine planes carrying men of H-Company dumped their troopers some nine miles from their intended drop zone. They did not know it then, but this was a sign of what would take place one month later when they dropped into Normandy.

As the days drew closer and closer to the invasion, the men were moved from their base camps to the marshalling areas. Once in the marshalling areas the soldiers were cut off from the rest of the world for security reasons. Here they received the equipment needed for the invasion, and waited for their final orders. Those orders came, and the men of deuce now understood what the previous months' training was all about. The Normandy mission for the 502nd 3rd Battalion was to seize and secure exits 3 and 4, the two northern exits behind Utah Beach. 1st and 2nd Battalions of the deuce were to knock out four concrete German 122mm howitzer gun positions near exit 4, at Saint Martin-de-Varreville, to prevent them from being used against the beach forces that would land that morning.[1]

The 377th Parachute Field Artillery Battalion

The 377th PFAB, which supported the 502nd PIR, was at this time the sole parachute cannoneer unit in the 101st. It was scattered and frustrated in its intentions on D-Day. Early on, just one of its pack 75s could be put into action. Five more were pulled out of the muck and mire, but proved incomplete or damaged.

506th Parachute Infantry Regiment

On 20 July 1942 the 506th PIR was activated, and Lt. Col. Robert F. Sink was named regimental commander. Lt. Col. Sink, who had been a member of the original 501st Parachute Infantry Battalion, relinquished his command of the 503rd PIR to Lt. Col. Kenneth Kinsler, and immediately began the task of thoroughly conditioning his new recruits. Like many of the airborne regimental commanders of his day, Col. "Bounding Bob" Sink instilled his own unique style of leadership on his troops, who took their training camp reviews on the double. Besides setting a world record, this demanding style of training would serve the men well during the war, when they were renowned for marching great distances in short periods of time.

This training took place in Camp Toccoa, Georgia, which was adjacent to the Currahee Mountains. Ironically "Currahee" meant "stand alone" in the local Indian language, and the troopers immediately adopted it as their regimental motto, since that was their objective behind enemy lines.

Towards the end of November 1942, the 506th PIR was ordered to Fort Benning for parachute training. Upon arrival at Fort Benning, the 506th immediately started their parachute training. They learned to pack their own chutes, and to prepare their equipment to be dropped in an airborne operation. Once their advanced airborne training at Fort Benning was completed, the unit moved to Camp Mackall, N.C. It was here that extensive tactical training was conducted, including many night jumps.

The 506th PIR was attached to the 101st Airborne Division on 1 June 1943. Later that month the regiment moved west to participate in the Tenessee maneuvers. After participating in the maneuvers, the 506th moved to Fort Bragg, N.C., until the end of August 1943, when the unit reported to Camp Shanks, N.Y., to prepare to be transported overseas. The 506th crossed the Atlantic

Details of a paratrooper's equipment from the 506th PIR. He is armed with a breakdown M-1 A1 rifle. (Nara)

506th PIR Patch, British made. (Coll. B. Foucher)

on the *SS Samaria* during September, arriving at Liverpool, England, on 15 September 1943.

In England, the 506th was stationed in the County of Wiltshire, with units in such villages as Aldbourne, Ramsbury, Floxfield, and Chilton-Foliat. Here the unit took part in such exercises as "Operation Wadham and Rankin" in preparation for the coming invasion of occupied Europe. June 5th, 1944, found the men of the 506th stationed by the aircraft that were to carry them into their first combat mission.[2]

Glider troops

The 327th Glider Infantry Regiment

The 327th was originally organized as an infantry regiment in the summer of 1942 as part of the 82nd Infantry Division at Camp Claiborne, Louisiana. As the airborne concept was pushed into further development because of the coming of war, the 82nd was chosen to become the first of four airborne divisions to be created during World War II. During the final days of the unit's basic training, the men were told by their commander, Major General Omar N. Bradley, that the Division was to be split to form a second Division, the 101st. Furthermore, he informed the men that the two divisions were to be airborne, and the 327th was to be trained as Glider Infantry. The men were not sure about flying in gliders. Most of them had never even flown in a plane. Some men went AWOL, to return after a few days, but all knew that war was approaching, and that they had to fight for their country. On 15 August 1942 the 327th Infantry became a Glider Infantry Regiment, and was reassigned to the newly formed 101st Airborne Division. The Glider Regiments had previously consisted of two battalions each. Upon reorganization they consisted of three battalions each. The 401st Glider Infantry Regiment—a sister regiment—was deactivated, and transferred its First Battalion to the 327th (later the battalion would be consolidated and redesignated as the 3rd Battalion, 327th Glider Infantry). In the fall of 1942 the two regiments headed to Fort Bragg, N.C., to begin training with the CG-4a Glider. Along the way the glidermen were introduced to the paratroopers of the 502nd PIR. Many fights would break out between these two groups, as the paratroopers thought they were the best, and that the glidertroopers did not have the "Right Stuff" to be Airborne Soldiers. Nevertheless, in North Carolina the men received glider training at Laurinburg-Maxton Army Air Base. The first flights caused ill effects on some of the men, who used their helmets, since airsickness bags were not available at the time. As training with the gliders progressed it became more apparent that landing men by gliders was more dangerous than landing by parachute. Some of the landings were to result in serious injuries, mostly broken arms and legs. On landing, gliders would slide out of control and crash into trees or fences. Some, upon landing, would slide in, and the nose of the glider would dig in and cause it to tilt up vertically on its nose section, causing the contents of the glider to break free of its lashing and come crashing forward, injuring glidermen and glider pilots alike.

The 401st Glider Infantry Regiment

The 401st Infantry Regiment was constitued on March 12th, 1918, but was never called to active service. On June 24th, 1921, the regiment was assigned to the 101st Infantry Division as organized

April 1944, England: the Waco gliders arrive at English airbases. (NARA)

reserves. Since the 101st Infantry Division was already an established division on paper and had a basic structure, it was chosen to become the second airborne division. Consequently, the 401st was deactivated as an infantry regiment on August 15th, 1942, and reconstitued on August 16th, 1942, as an Airborne Infantry Regiment at Camp Claiborne, LA. It consisted of two battalions that would land in gliders or by transport aircrafts into a landing zone secured by paratroop forces.

The 401st would train at posts in the southern and southeastern United States, including Fort Bragg, SC, until July 1943, when they would be transferred to the embarkation area in New York. On September 4th, under the command of Lt. Colonel Ray C. Allen, the 401st was deployed to England aboard the British ship HMS *Strathnaver*, landing at Liverpool, England. From Liverpool the 401st began to move into the war area. Riding on a blacked-out train in the middle of the night the glidermen could, for the first time, hear bombs exploding in the distance. Their destination, reached about dawn, was Reading, a town in southern England, in Berkshire—only 35 miles from London. Here the 401st went into camp. Their new base was Brock Barracks, the home of the Royal Berkshire Regiment. In England the training continued with exercises BEAVER, TIGER, and EAGLE in preparation for the invasion of Europe. In exercise Tiger, the glidermen had a chance to train for their function in this new capacity. In March 1944 the 401st was separated. The 1st Battalion would stay with the 101st Airborne Division, but would be sent to the 327th GIR as the 3rd Battalion. The 2nd Battalion would go to the 82nd Airborne Division, 325th GIR, as the 3rd Battalion. While the 1st Battalion of the 401st would frequently serve with the 327th, its assignment for Normandy was to be part of Division reserve. It would come in by sea with the 4th Infantry Division.

For the D-Day Invasion (Operation Neptune) on June 6th, 1944, the 1-401st arrived on UTAH Beach with the 4th Infantry Division in the UNCLE RED sector. It was to link up with the paratroopers that landed earlier that morning. On June 7th the 401st fought several engagements in an effort to join Colonel Bob Sink's 506'rs march on St. Come-du-Mont. It was during this time the unit suffered its first casualties. Among the casualties was Captain McDonald's Company XO, Lieutenant Joe O'Brien, whose grenade apparently detonated. Just before midnight the battalion at last contacted Colonel Sink's 506'rs near Angoville-au-Plain. While in the assembly area the Protestant Chaplain, Captain John R. Steel, had commented to Colonel Allen, "It's just like maneuvers, except we have been issued live ammunitions." During the night Captain Steel was mistaken for a German infiltrator, and was shot and killed by a member of the unit.

Colonel Allen, who had been a Texas National Guard Officer, was renowned for being an aggressive commander. He immediately contacted Colonel Sink for orders. It was around midnight, and Colonel Sink had already retired, but gave his orders for the early morning attack across the Douve River on June 8th from his sleeping bag. Immediately Allen called his company commanders together and issued orders for the attack.

The morning of June 8th found the 401st spread out along the west bank of the Douve. Company C of the 1st Battalion, commanded by Captain Robert Galbraith, led the assault across the river after dark, followed by the rest of the 1st Battalion. Once the 1/401st was linked to the 101st it would aid in the capture of Sainte Come-du-Mont that evening, as well as Carentan on June 15th, after five days of bitter combat. Later, the 1/401st would join the VII Corps on Utah Beach and the V Corps on Omaha Beach when they met forces of the 175th Regiment 4th Infantry Division in the town of Auville-sur-le-Vey.

The 321st Glider Field Artillery Battalion

During the third month of World War II, the 321st Field Artillery was reorganized and redesignated on 13 February 1942 as Battery C, 321st Field Artillery Battalion, before being ordered into active military service on 25 March 1942 at Camp Claiborne, LA. It was once again reorganized and redisignated on 15 August 1942 as Battery C, 321st Glider Field Artillery Battalion—an element of the 101st Airborne Division—with Lieutenant Colonel Edward L. Carmichael assuming command of the battalion upon its reactivation.

The 321st GFAB initially landed on Utah Beach on D-Day aboard the Liberty ship *John S. Mosby*, but were unable to engage in any action for several days. The reason for this was the division of the battalion into two groups. The second group was aboard the *Susan B. Anthony*, which struck a mine and sank off Omaha Beach. The artillery troopers managed to get ashore without loss of life; however, they had to wait until June 9th for the guns and vehicles to be off-loaded. During this time part of the battalion served as forward observers for the 506th PIR, directing naval and self-propelled 105mm fire.

By 9 June 1944 the 321st were firing in support of a coordinated offensive action undertaken by the 327th GIR as they crossed the Douve River.

The 321st continued offensive operations supporting the 327th GIR throughout this early campaign. Once across the Douve, the 321st set up its guns near Catz, laying fire on the far banks of the canal. It was relieved of action on 10 July 1944, and sailed for the base camp in England aboard an LST on 13 July 1944.

The 326th Airborne Engineer Battalion

The 326th Engineers were constitued in the National Army on 23 July 1918 as an element of the 101st Division. The unit was demobilized on 11 December 1918. It was reconstitued on 24 June 1921 as the 326th Engineers (Combat), an element of the 101st Division in Organized Reserves, and reconstitued in November 1921 at Milwaukee, Wisconsin.

The regiment was divided on 31 March 1942. All Regimental units (less the 2d Battalion) were alloted to the Army of the United States on 15 August 1942. At that time they were redesignated as the 326th Airborne Engineer Battalion (AEB), and were activated at Camp Clairborne, LA. The battalion moved to Fort Bragg, NC, with the 101st Airborne Division on 29 September 1942. The battalion participated in all division exercises and maneuvers.

After extensive training in the United States, the 326th AEB deployed to England on 5 September 1943, from Pier 90, North River, New York. Ship 294 (HMS *Samaria*) landed at Liverpool, England, and the battalion moved by train to Basildon Park, near Reading, Berkshire. Under the command of Lieutenant Colonel John Pappas, the Battalion's training focused on physical conditioning (including long and short marches), firing of weapons, glider loading, glider flights, and unit and division tactical exercises. The 326th AEB participated in the airborne assault into Normandy, where Lieutenant Colonel John Pappas was killed in action on 13 June 1944. Major Hugh A. Moseley assumed command, and led the battalion during Operation Market Garden, as well as during the Screaming Eagles' heroic stand at Bastogne.

The 907th Glider Field Artillery Battalion

The 307th Ammunition Train was constitued on 5 August 1917 as part of the National Army at Camp Gordon, near Atlanta, GA, and assigned to the 82nd Infantry Division. The unit saw extensive action in World War I during the Lorraine Campaign, and the St. Mihiel and Meuse-Argonne Offensives. It was demobilized 18-23 May 1919 at Camp Upton, NY, then reconstitued 24 June 1921 in the Organized Reserves and assigned to the 82nd Infantry Division.

In January 1942 the 307th Ammunition Train was redisignated the 907th Glider Field Artillery Battalion, then reactivated 2 months later on 25 March 1942 at Camp Claiborne, LA, under the command of Lieutenant Colonel Clarence F. Nelson, who would lead the battalion until its deactivation after World War II.

After intensive training at Camp Claiborne, LA, the 907th Glider Field Artillery Battalion—now an element of the 101st Airborne Division—began moving to staging areas on 22 August 1943 at Camp Shanks, NY, with the rest of the division for overseas deployment. On 4 September the 907th set sail for England aboard the *SS Strathnaver* and arrived at Liverpool, England, on 18 October. After moving inland the 907th eventually set up encampment at Benham Valence, near Newbury, and adopted the unit code name Kite. The battalion participated in Exercise Tiger, which was staged during the week of April 23-30, 1944, as a rehearsal of the opening phase of the Utah Beach landings under VII Corps auspices.

The 907th GFAB, along with a group of the 321st GFAB, were aboard the *Susan B. Anthony*, which struck a mine and sank off Omaha Beach. A small echelon of the 907th GFAB consisting of an officer and three enlisted men did parachute onto the DZ on D-Day, however, the main body of the battalion arrived seaborne.

By 10 June 1944 the 907th was firing in support of a coordinated offensive action undertaken by the 502nd PIR in the general vicinity of St. Come-du-Mont.

The 907th continued offensive operations, supporting the 502nd and 501st PIRs throughout this early campaign. On 26 June the battalion took up tactical bivouac positions west of St-Sauveur-le-Vicomte along with the 501st PIR, and eventually moved to Tollevast, south of Cherbourg, with the rest of the 101st, where they patrolled the area. It was relieved from action on 10 July 1944 and sailed for the base camp in England aboard an LST on 13 July 1944.

Special troops

The 81st Airborne Anti-Aircraft Battalion (AAA)

The 81st Airborne Anti-Aircraft Battalion was activated on 4 September 1942 by General Order #8, HQ 101st Airborne Division, at Camp Claiborne, LA. The battalion, commanded by Lieutenant Colonel W.C. Scoggin, was a special troop unit of the 101st Airborne Division, and was activated from units of the 401st and 327th Glider Infantry Regiments. All personnel were infantry trained.

The 3rd Battalion of the 401st Glider Infantry, less Company K, was transferred to the 81st Battalion, with I and L Companies becoming Battery C and F. Company B of the 327th Glider Infantry became Battery B of the 81st. The first and second platoons of the anti-tank companies of the 327th Glider Infantry became Battery A, 81st Battalion. The heavy weapons Companies H and E of the 327th Glider Infantry became Battery D and E, 81st Battalion. The Headquarters Detachment came from Headquarters Company, 1st Battalion, 327th GIR, via Headquarters Company, 3rd Battalion, 401st GIR. The Medical Detachment was composed of medical personnel from the 327th and 401st GIR, 326th and 325th Airborne Medical Companies.

All personnel above the T/O of 71 men per battery; 23 men of Medical Detachment and 26 men of Headquarters Detachment were transferred out to other units of the division. Batteries A, B, and C were anti-tank batteries, each with eight 37mm A/T guns, which were changed to 57mm gun, and then to the British six pound guns for combat, as they were more suited to gliders. Batteries D, E, and F were anti-aircraft batteries, each with 12 50 caliber air-cooled machine guns on M-3 mounts. After Normandy, ground mounts were secured so the guns could be fired as ground weapons to support the infantry units of the division, who had only 30 caliber air-cooled machine guns.

The battalion moved to Fort Bragg, NC, with the division on 29 September 1942. Training began on the new weapons, loading of gliders, taking glider flights, and unloading the gliders. The battalion participated in all division exercises and maneuvers. The division was scheduled to sail for England 5 September 1943, from Pier 90, North River, NY. The battalion was assigned as an advanced party to the ship to furnish all fatigue details, ship security, and manning the ship's AA guns, with Lieutenant Colonel Scoggin as commander of troops aboard ship.

Ship 294 (HMS *Samaria*) landed at Liverpool, England, and the battalion moved by train to Basildon Park, near Reading, Berkshire. Training was intensified on physical training, firing of weapons, glider loading, glider flights, and unit and division tactical exercises. On 25 March 1944 Lieutenant Colonel Scoggin was transferred, and Lieutenant Colonel X.B. Cox, Jr., was given command of the battalion, and remained in command for the duration.

On 6 June 1944 Batteries A and B were air lifted by glider to Normandy, where they landed at H+2 hours. Batteries D, E, and F came in by sea, with the assault wave of engineers and infantrymen of the 8th Infantry Regiment, 4th Infantry Division landing at H+15 minutes. They set up the first anti-aircraft protection on the beach, and remained in that position until 11 June, when they were released by 7th Corps and returned to battalion control, to enable them to set up AA protection for division headquarters and major bridges around Carentan. The batteries were given credit for destroying at least two enemy planes during 6-7 June.

3

Four Years of Occupation in Normandy 1940-1944

Within a few months—from summer 1939 to spring 1940—the lives of the people living in the County of Manche changed radically: while they were living a rather carefree life, they now had to experience terror, prohibitions, restrictions, frustrations and resentment, as well as hopes and compromises. These many trying circumstances, and the strong feelings that resulted explain how after four years of "Occupation" the landing was seen as "Liberation."

23 August 1939

On the Napoleon Beach, the bathers enjoyed the summer sun that shone on Cherbourg. A summer like any other? Not really. On the same day, Hitler's Germany and Stalin's Russia signed the Nazi Soviet Pact, which stipulated a mutual non-agression, and had already agreed on the future partition of Poland.

The news hit Europe like a bombshell. In Cherbourg, people could already feel the effects of this devastating news. The first recruitment of staff was set up to welcome the reservists. At the transatlantic terminal, the crew of the German steamship

Bremen rushed on the newspapers to read the news and the comments before leaving for New York. The Bremen would never be seen again on Quay de France, nor would any German steamship....

Mobilizations were ordered the week after, first only for men who were old enough to be drafted. In the County of Manche, about 45,000 men were called up. Hundreds of them arrived every day at the mobilization center in Cherbourg in a great confusion, some of them with their wives and children. As there was no room left to quarter the new arrivals, schools and Parish rooms were requisitioned, and wood barracks were built hastily on Divette square. At the military shipyard, the pace was so much quickened that the management had to call back retired workers. On 26 and 27 August, the first battalions of the 8th and 11th Infantry Regiments left for Rouen and Lens. The civilians summoned up their energy; the mayor of Cherbourg listed all the shelters in town (three in total, in which only 1,300 people could take cover), and the trenches to be dug to shelter the rest of the population. Some had already stocked supplies. Finally, the local savings bank was taken by storm: 3.2 million francs were withdrawn within a month, whereas only 1.9 million francs were deposited. Worried about the future perhaps?

On the evening of 31 August the people of Manche went to sleep in a world that was on watch, but still in peace. Yet the night was short. At daybreak on 1 September, Germany and Russia invaded Poland. From then on the events went faster. On 2 September, France began general mobilizations. The day after, France and Great Britain declared war on Germany. Since the political scene was tense, the *Cherbourg-Eclair* newspaper got into the habit of sticking up the latest news as it arrived, on Place du Ch,teau; people seemed to receive the news quietly. The bell tolled in the countryside. Some of the soldiers of the 1914 War (WWI) hid to cry. Some others recovered the same old reflexes as 25 years before, and shouted "To Berlin!"

Berlin? At that moment, "To Cherbourg" would have been more accurate. For the war that had just been declared had nothing to do with the last one, whether the nostalgic people liked it or not. Cherbourg, several hundreds of miles from the German frontier; Cherbourg, with its military shipyard and its military harbour; Cherbourg could, from then on, be considered a potential target for the enemy's air force. This theory was confirmed no later than 4 September, when the air-raid siren screamed suddenly during the market.

The following eight months were a strange period. France was at war, but her soldiers were hidden behind the Maginot Line, waiting for the Germans, themselves hidden behind the Siegfried

Line. Few or no fights, and "Quiet days on the whole front"—the official statement from headquarters summed up the situation perfectly.

In Cherbourg, the civil authorities tried to "educate" the population in civil defense: no light during the night, and adhesive tape on the windows to prevent them from smashing to pieces at the first explosion.

When the Germans attacked on 10 May, and crushed the French Army within the next days in Sedan and Dinant; the people from Cherbourg and Manche could not believe it. Within a week the tune changed radicaly. The Mayor of Cherbourg urged his fellow citizens:

"No ifs or buts anymore. Dig some trenches in your gardens, even if they're only one yard in depth. Shore up your cellars. Build some shelters with bags filled with sand. A bad shelter is better than no shelter at all."

At 8:15 PM on June 17th, the Germans were reported to be in Villedieu; a quarter of an hour later they were in Coutances (where a few inhabitants, thinking they were British, applauded when they passed!), and a little later in Lessay.

On 18 June the Germans stood at Cherbourg's doors. There were still fights in Martinvast, at Le Roule, and at the Fort of Querqueville, while at the military shipyard a few workers sabotaged the submarines on their building stocks. On 19 June, after a brush with the worst (a bombardement of the town) and a last stand, the Cherbourg garrison surrendered. At 2:30 PM the fights stopped officially. The people of Cherbourg, who had left in droves during the last days, could come back home. The department could count its dead and wounded: 1,000 killed during the French campaign, and 4,000 wounded. 20,000 people of Manche were taken prisoners.

The Occupation started.

Very quickly, the County of Manche realized how heavy the weight of Occupation would be. First of all, the anticipation of what might happen: from then on, the country lived according to German rules, and had to obey the curfew. In town, the passers-by had to draw aside to let the officers pass. In Cherbourg, the pavements on the left were reserved for the Germans, and people had to "cross the streets by the shortest way, in a straight line." Listening to the BBC, and hiding or owning arms or carrier pigeons were forbidden. Dances were prohibited.

People had to have a pass to get out of their towns. In October 1941 a coastal zone was created, including the whole littoral of the county, to which access was drastically controlled. Six months later, the whole region of La Hague was declared a prohibited area for any person who did not live in it.

People also had to put up with an intrusive German presence. Next to England, Manche was considered an important strategic position, and it "welcomed" many German units, which had to be fed and quartered. The people felt the Wehrmacht was robbing them: a wealthy region, the County of Manche supplied the German cooks with hundreds of tons of meat, milk, butter, and vegetables. And the soldiers had no scruples over entering a shop, a farm, or a restaurant, and guzzling and taking everything for free.

The officers were quartered in the castles, manors, and hotels; the non-commisionned officers and the troops were in private houses, or in schools. This forced cohabitation was an insult to the people's pride, with almost nothing offered in return: 5 francs of compensation per day for an officer, 3 francs for a soldier.

At the beginning of autumn 1940, the ration of meat per person was 360 grams a week. It went down to 120 grams in April 1943. Same shortage on potatoes, butter, pasta, shoes, clothes, and coal; everything was rationed, because there was a lack of everything. In the countryside people went on eating their fill (even making good bargains sometimes). The people in town wanted to fill their plates, and their stomachs had to face hardships with resignation.

1942, Valognes: The Germans have requisitioned all the horses. The Normans must hand them over to the enemy. (D. François)

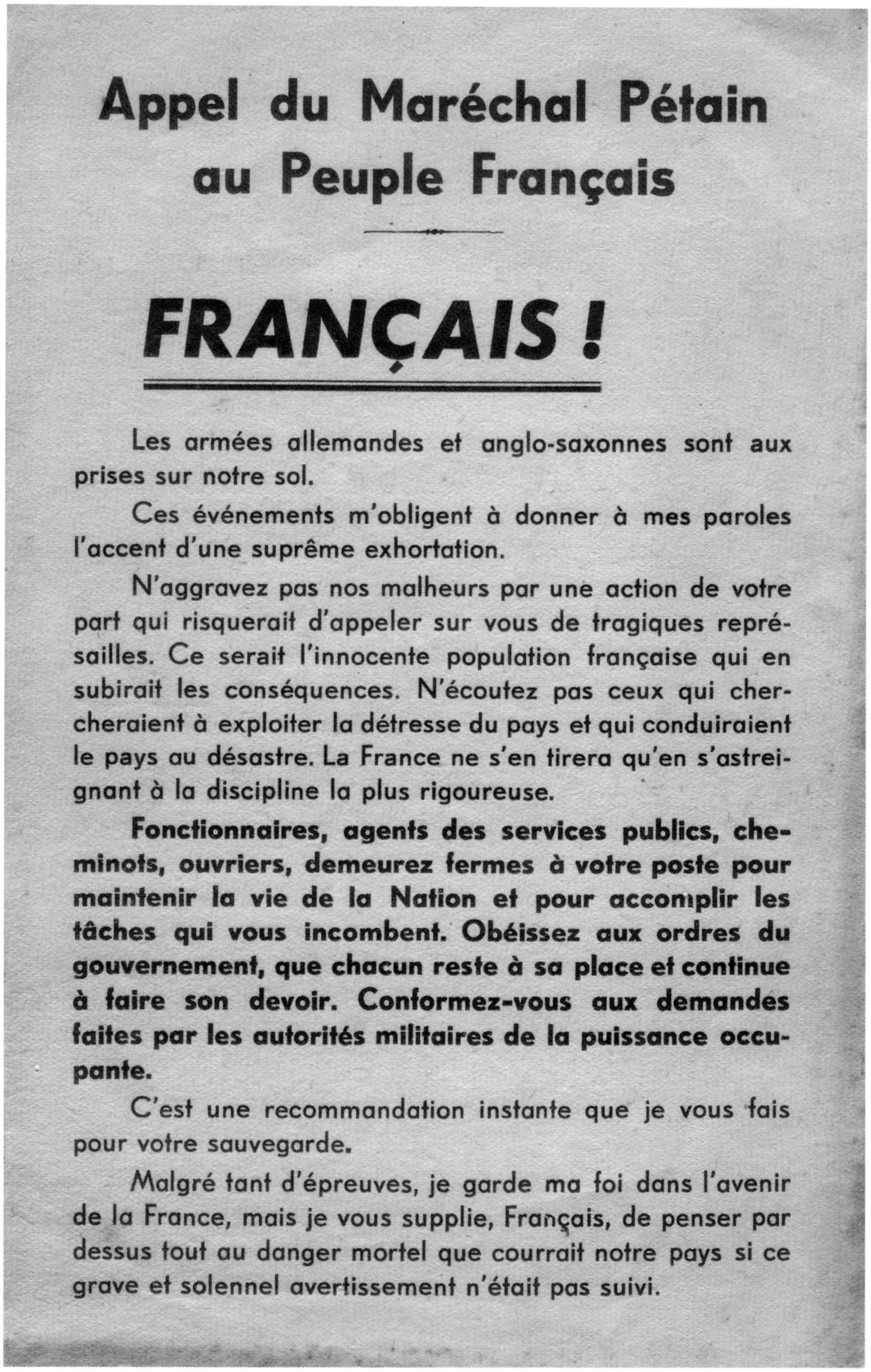

Appel du Maréchal Pétain au Peuple Français

FRANÇAIS !

Les armées allemandes et anglo-saxonnes sont aux prises sur notre sol.

Ces événements m'obligent à donner à mes paroles l'accent d'une suprême exhortation.

N'aggravez pas nos malheurs par une action de votre part qui risquerait d'appeler sur vous de tragiques représailles. Ce serait l'innocente population française qui en subirait les conséquences. N'écoutez pas ceux qui chercheraient à exploiter la détresse du pays et qui conduiraient le pays au désastre. La France ne s'en tirera qu'en s'astreignant à la discipline la plus rigoureuse.

Fonctionnaires, agents des services publics, cheminots, ouvriers, demeurez fermes à votre poste pour maintenir la vie de la Nation et pour accomplir les tâches qui vous incombent. Obéissez aux ordres du gouvernement, que chacun reste à sa place et continue à faire son devoir. Conformez-vous aux demandes faites par les autorités militaires de la puissance occupante.

C'est une recommandation instante que je vous fais pour votre sauvegarde.

Malgré tant d'épreuves, je garde ma foi dans l'avenir de la France, mais je vous supplie, Français, de penser par dessus tout au danger mortel que courrait notre pays si ce grave et solennel avertissement n'était pas suivi.

1940: The Government of Général Pétain has asked all Frenchmen to stop fighting.

The Occupation lasted for four years in Manche. Too long for most of its inhabitants, fed up with tightening their belts and living with fear all the time. One can be sure that the people from the county of Manche, like the vast majority of the French population, were waiting impatiently for the arrival of the Allied troops in their country. This impatience was all the greater now that the German's luck had turned since 1940. The Germans, who used to dominate the situation, were now on the defensive in Italy and in Russia. A third front in Western Europe would make them fall into a trap. A landing? Certainly. But where and when would this great landing happen? Nobody knew.

4

Neptune Operation

On 8 May the Supreme Commander Allied Forces Europe, General Dwight D. Eisenhower, designated D-Day as 5 June, but as the day for the invasion of France drew near, a bad weather forecast caused the assault on the Normandy coastline to be postponed until the following day. Some 2,876,000 men were ready to cross the English Channel for the greatest seaborne military operation in history, with over 20,000 invasion troops being scheduled to go ashore from ships and craft on D-Day.

Starting at 6:30 AM on 6 June the U.S. 1st Army was due to land on the right of the line on the Cotentin peninsula, southeast of Cherbourg on "Utah," and further east on "Omaha" beaches, while the British 2nd Army (including the Canadian 3rd Division) would land 50 minutes later on the left on "Gold," "Juno," and "Sword" beaches.

The American attack was to be spearheaded by the U.S. 82nd and 101st Airborne Divisions, which landed shortly after midnight astride the Merderet River, in the vicinity of Sainte-Mere-Eglise and Carentan, in order to facilate the advance of the U.S. VII Corps. At the same time the British 6th Airborne Division, landing 40 miles to the east, was to secure the Allied left flank between the Orne and Dives Rivers.

The U.S. 1st Army commander, Lieutenant General Omar N. Bradley, planned to use the 82nd and 101st Airborne Divisions to ensure success during the "Utah" beach landings, and to seal off the main roads leading in and out of the Cotentin peninsula. His plan was to drop both divisions along the base (or neck) of the peninsula, where they were to key into the Douve River, which slices accross two-thirds of the neck. The American airborne troops were to put a stranglehold on the huge peninsula, cutting off routes of supply and escape to thousands of Germans troops stationed there. Bradley assigned to the 101st Airborne Division the mission of landing by parachute and glider behind "Utah" beach. A small patrol (one officer and six men of the British 1st S.A.S. regiment) was also to be dropped south of Carentan to assist the 101st by creating diversions with pyrotechnics.

The first and most important objectives were the four exits from the beach, codenamed Utah, which the American 4th Division would need when they moved inland from their landing places. Because the coast was low and marshy, these exits on to dry ground were each about a mile from high-water mark, at Pouppeville (Exit 1), Hébert (Exit 2), Audouville-la-Hubert (Exit 3), and Saint Martin-de-Varreville (Exit 4). From Pouppeville, along the estuary of the Douve, the objectives were a series of locks across the river, which the parachutists were to seize and hold so that they might be used for moving between Utah beachhead and the Omaha beachhead to the east when the time came to join the two. The objectives along the course of the Douve were also a series of crossing places, some of which were to be destroyed to deny their use to the Germans, while others were to be held either for the immediate use of the parachutists, or for a break-out later by the beach-landed infantry and armour. The most important of these were, from east to west, Saint Côme-du-Mont, Chef-du-Pont, and Pont l'Abbé. Thereafter the line of objectives, from Pont l'Abbé back to Exit 4, ran through the open countryside, and would have to be defended, if and when captured, by grit and hope.

The danger to this open flank would come, it was believed, from the two German divisions that were known to have long been stationed in Cotentin—the 709th on the east coast and the 243rd on the west—and the recently arrived 91st, which had unfortunately been positioned exactly astride of the airborne area. Moreover, while the 709th and 243rd were static formations—what the Germans called *bodenst‰ndige* ("ground holding"), a euphemistic admission of their total lack of mechanical transport and the low physical fitness of their soldiers—the 91st was composed of young men who had actually been trained in air movement. Still, between them they fielded no more than 24 battalions against the 18 that the Americans could parachute. Moreover, several of the German battalions were not German at all in composition, but manned by more-or-less willing volunteers from the army of prisoners the Germans had taken in the east during 1941-42. They were indeed known as East (*Ost*) Battalions, but to have called them Russian would have been inaccurate. They represented, for the most part, the peripheral and unassimilated people of the Russian empire: Cossacks, Georgians, Turkomen, Armenians, Volga Tartars, and Azerbaijanis, who had swapped a tenuous sense of citizenship for the guarantee of regular meals, and might be expected to waver in their new loyalty if pressed to fight for their suppers. That prospect rather bettered the odds, which the Americans calculated to yield a more or less even fight on the first day, when most of the defenders would be pinned in their fixed positions. At worst, it was thought, the Germans would be able to find five battalions to mount a counterattack against the parachutists, and to concentrate no armour against them until the third day. The forecast was slightly optimistic. There was also in the area a scratch panzer battalion, No. 100, equipped with old French tanks and makeshift assault guns, and the 6th Parachute Regiment, for a combined total of three battalions of highly trained soldiers, whose average age was 17 1/2 (it was 36 in the 709th Division).

German Troops in Lower Normandy

716th Infantry Division: positioned from the mouth of the Orne to Arromanches, this 8,000-strong unit was under the command of General Richter.

352nd Infantry Division: this was a unit of 12,000 experienced troops that had previously fought in Russia. It occupied the sector from Arromanches to the mouth of the Vire, and was commanded by General Kraiss.

709th Infantry Division: Its mission was to defend the Cotentin Peninsula, under General Von Schlieben. But motivation levels were low for its 12,600 men.

91st Infantry Division: brought in as reserves to the La Haye-du-Puits/Saint-Sauveur-le-Vicomte sector. General Falley was in command of this 10,000-man division.

6th Parachute Regiment: 3,500 elite troops, young and highly motivated, under the orders of General Von der Heydte. Based at Lessay/Carentan.

Reserve troops (armored divisions)

PanzerLehr Division: 16,000 men and 260 tanks stationed around Chartes/Orléans/Le Mans.

12th SS "Hitlerjugend" Division: 20,000 men and 200 tanks stationed around Evreux/Elbeuf.

21st Panzer Division: 16,000 men and 170 tanks stationed at Caen/St Pierre-sur-Dives.

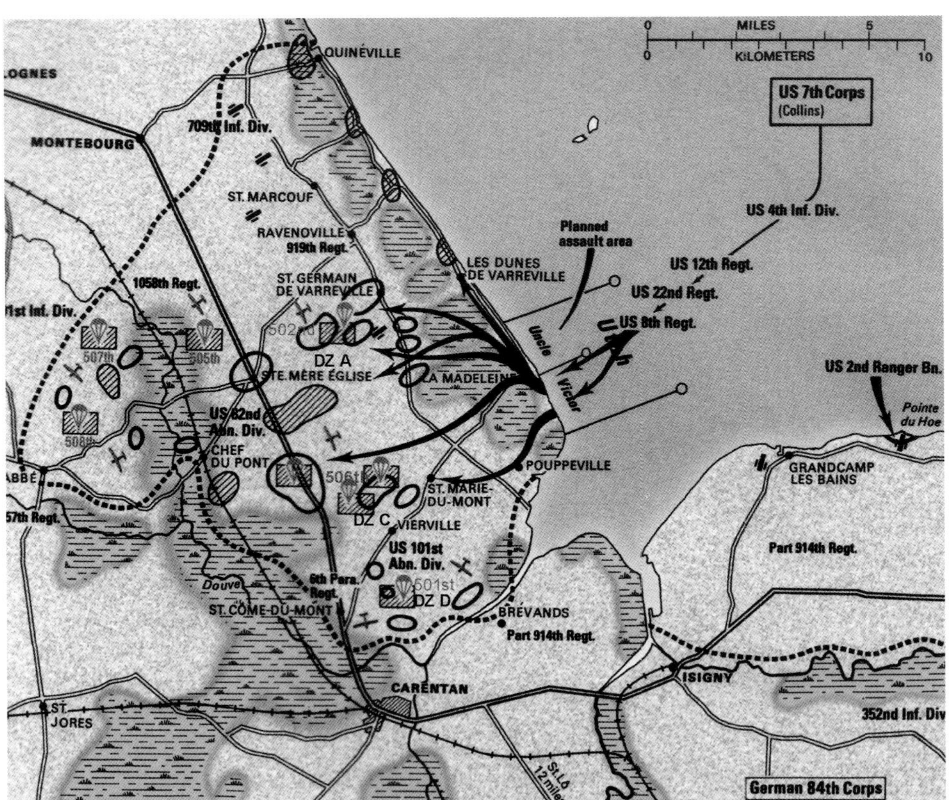

5 June, 1944: Ike meets with the paratroopers of the 502nd PIR before they board for Normandy. (NARA)

Ike pays a call on E Company, 502nd PIR at Greenham Common, 5 June, 1944. Lieutenant Wallace Stobel on the right. (NARA)

506th demo men Clarence Ware and Charles Plaudo applying "warpaint." Ware was wounded on D-Day between St. Côme-du-Mont and the bridges at La Barquette. (NARA)

Before Operation Overlord, the morale of the troops is very high. (NARA)

T/4 Joseph Gorenc, HHC, 506th PIR, June 5 1944. (Nara)

23 March 1944: The British Prime Minister watches a massive airdrop. (NARA)

In addition to folding parachutes, the "Rigger" was responsible for repairing and modifying all equipment specific to parachutes. (NARA)

The T-5 parachutes are stored in kit-bags for Operation Neptune. More than 13,000 parachutes will be needed for this airborne operation. (NARA)

These paratroopers have received their reinforced jumpsuits a few days before D-Day. (NARA)

In England, the "riggers" are busy folding the thousands of parachutes that will be needed for Operation Neptune. (NARA)

Winston Churchill, flanked by Generals Eisenhower and Taylor, visits the airborne troops who will, in a few months, open a third front in Europe. (NARA)

Left: This paratrooper has radio equipment. Below: These airborne artillerymen prepare containers for the shells that will be transported by glider. (NARA)

5 June 1944: These paratroopers with blackened faces write one last letter before leaving for Normandy. (NARA)

These paratroopers show different expressions on their faces before the big jump. This will be the first combat for the troopers of the 101st Airborne Division. (NARA)

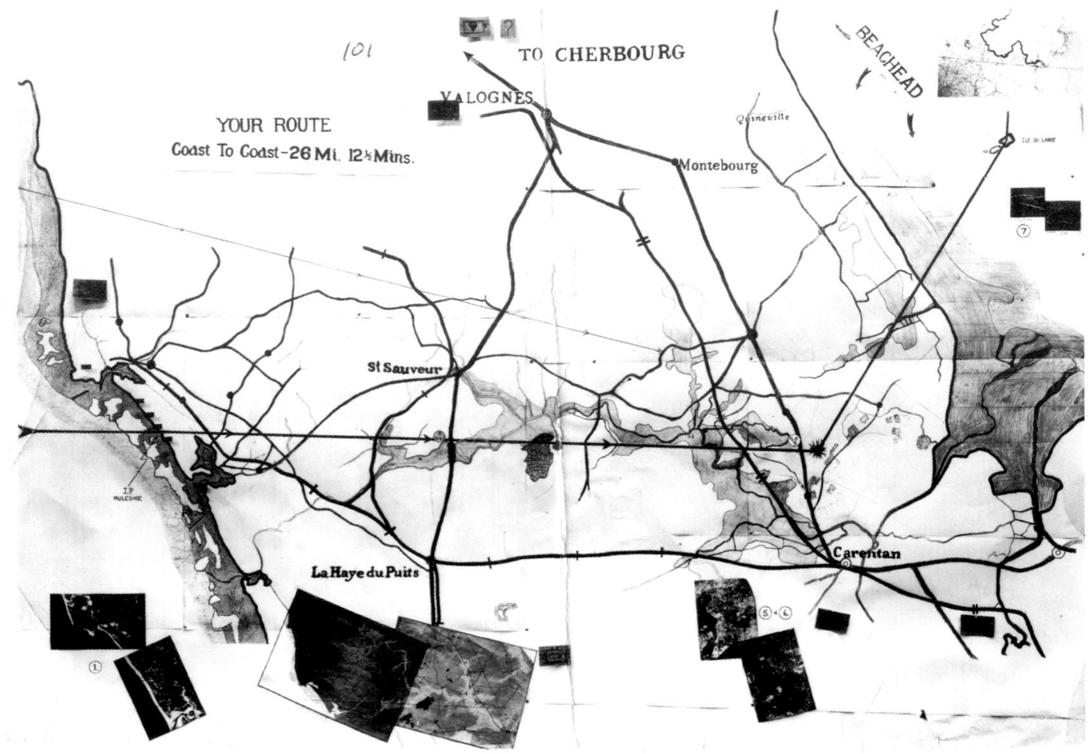

Photograph given to the officers of the airborne troops of the 101st Division before D-Day; it shows the roads and the landmarks that will lead them to the jump sight. (NARA)

Before D-Day, American troops learning to handle enemy weapons. Here, an MG-42. (NARA)

The paratroopers of the 101st Airborne Division embark in the C-47 for Operation Neptune.

Practicing to shoot the German MG-34 machine gun. (NARA)

Using the Mauser G-98 rifle. (NARA)

Firing the P-08 Luger pistol. (NARA)

Colonel Robert Sink, 506th PIR (right), discusses matters of mutual interest with his USAAF counterpart, Colonel Charles Young. (NARA)

LTC. Wolverton, June 5th 1944. (NARA)

5 June 1944, on the airfields in the South of England: Thousands of planes transporting troops and gliders wait for the cover of darkness to take off for Normandy. (NARA)

The men of the 327th Glider Infantry Regiment land at Utah Beach, and will make up the Seaborne.

6 June: Men of the 101st Airborne Division land at Utah Beach. On the right, a US M1-A1 rifle.

Stick of paratroopers of the 101st Airborne during a jump in England, a few weeks before the Landings. (NARA)

June 5, 1944: Screaming Eagles take part in a Protestant prayer service aboard a landing craft delivering them to Normandy for the D-Day Invasion. (NARA)

Pathfinders

The commanders of both the troops' carrier and airborne units decided to form a combined service organization to carry out future pathfinder operations. In early 1944, a new unit was formed in England under command of the U.S. 9th Air Force. This new unit was designated the 9th Troop Carrier Pathfinder Group (Provisional). The group was to be commanded by then Lt. Colonel Joel L. Crouch, a well-seasoned C-47 pilot.

Many hours were spent training on navigational problems, night parachute jumps, and working with the equipment, which was new to most of the troops. By the middle of May 1944 the group was finished with its training, and was waiting for its first mission. It was at first believed that the group would be disbanded after the upcoming invasion of Europe, but the near future would show the need for a more permanent unit such as this.

It was not long of a wait before the invasion became a reality. On the evening of June 5, 1944, Lieutenant Colonel Crouch was at the controls of the C-47 leading the pathfinder group to its drop zones on the Cotentin Peninsula. Aboard this aircraft was Captain Frank Lillyman of the 502nd Parachute Infantry Regiment. Captain Lillyman was in command of the 101st Pathfinders, and jumped with his team on to Drop Zone A, just east of Sainte Mére Eglise. It is believed that Captain Lillyman was the first American paratrooper to land on French soil on D-Day.

It amounted to 19 men, including 101st Pathfinder OIC Captain Frank Lillyman, and three members of the regimental intelligence section charged with scouting the adversary's batteries at Saint-Martin de Varreville.

The most accurate Pathfinder drop in the 101st objective area put one team of the 506th PIR on Drop Zone C, and another within walking distance at Hiesville. Captain Lillyman's party had all three sticks close together—and a mile or more north of DZ "A," at Saint Germain de Varreville, where they hurriedly set up eurekas and lights. On DZ "D" the 501st Pathfinders found themselves landing under fire, and irretrievably involved in close combat from the moment they got out of their chutes.

I saw them jump to destiny

Ward Smith, war correspondant, flew with the men of the 101st Airborne Division in the plane that took them over Normandy. His report was published in the June 11th 1944 editions of the weekly *News of the World.*

This is the story of the first phase of the invasion as I saw it from the air in the early hours of D-Day at 1:40 AM. We were over Carentan, on the Cherbourg peninsula, in an American Ninth Troop-Carrier Command "leadership"...some 20 paratroops, the flying crew, and myself.

A moment later the plane was empty. The paratroops were making one of the initial descents of the second front, and the enemy from the ground was facing the finest shots of this most momentous of all campaigns

All around the plane, rocketing less than 100 feet from the ground a brock's benefit of flak rainbowed us for something like eight minutes on end by my watch, though I could have sworn it was at least half an hour.

It was dusk as our air fleet—the advance guard of the invasion—left an airport in England, and left twinkling lights for dark hazards.

So closely had the secret of D-Day been preserved that not all the flying crews themselves knew the signal had been given until they took off. The paratroops had been in barbed wire enclosures for some days. No one had chance to talk.

The previous day I had flown to London and back on urgent business. Immediately on my return I was summoned to a squadron Headquarters to sleep. But they did not show me my room; instead they led me right out to the airfield. To the first of a line of waiting planes, "This is it!" they remarked. It had come at last—just like that.

...As I climbed aboard paratroops, steel-helmeted, black-faced, and festooned from head to foot, were in their planes in the bucket seats lining each side of the fuselage. The co-pilot, Major Cannon, was reading a historic message from General Einsenhower. It spoke of the "Great Crusade," and ended:

'Let us beseech the blessing of Almighty God on this noble undertaking.'

As the door slanged to on us, sitting there in the dusk we realized that we had suddenly passed from one world to another. Perhaps that was partly the effect of the all-red lights in the plane. They made our faces look slightly blue. They turned white the red tips of our cigarettes. I think that perhaps all of us had a sinking feeling in the pit of our stomachs.

But that did not last long. Somehow we seemed to leave it behind on the ground.

Almost before we realized it we were off. Here and there lights, friendly lights, winked at us. Other planes, their red and green wing lights twinkling cheerfully, fell into close formation behind to left and right.

As everyone adjusted parachute harnesses, flak suits, and Mae Wests, our mood brightened to a spate of banter.

'Say,' someone sang out suddenly, 'What's the date? I'll feel kinda dumb down there if some guy asks me and I get it wrong.'

We laughed uproariously at things like that—the littlest things, the silliest things. We exchanged cigarettes and we talked on, but somehow never about things that mattered.

Among the paratroops were a doctor and two medical orderlies. They were going to drop with the rest to set up first-aid posts wherever opportunity offered. There was a chaplain, too.

While I was reflecting that I was certain to forget something, shore lights flashed in the distance. We could just make out land on the horizon under a glimmer of moon. The coast of France....

This was it—the Great Adventure everyone had lived for and worked for so long and so hard. Someone called out: 'Ten minutes to go.' I shall never forget the scene up there in those late, fateful minutes, those long lines of motionless, grim-faced young men burdened like pack horses so that they could hardly stand unaided. Just waiting...So young they looked, there on the edge of the unknown. And somehow so sad. They seemed to be asleep, but I could see lips moving wordlessly.

The jump door opened, letting in a dull red glare from the fires below. The time had come. We were over the drop zone. I wish I could play up that moment, but there was nothing to indicate that this was the supreme climax. Just a whistling that lasted for a few seconds—and those men, so young, so brave, had gone to their destinies. Then we got it. The Flak and tracers came up, from all sides. Through the still-open door at the side of the plane I could see it forming a blazing arch over us—an arch that lasted for minutes on end, and so close it seemed that we could not escape.

It felt very lonely up there then in that empty C-47. I think I sat on the floor. About the only thing I can be sure of is that I was bathed in perspiration....

101st Pathfinders. Frank Lillyman's group, first of the 101st Pathfinders. 502nd Parachute Infantry Pathfinder Team: back row, from left to right: First Lieutenant Samuel Mc Carter, First Lieutenant Robert S. Dixon, Private August M. Mangoni, Pvt. Bluford R.Williams, Pvt John S. Zamanakis, T-5 Owen R. Council, Pvt John H. Funk, S/S Thomas C.Walton, Pfc Delbert A. Jones, Front row, from left to right: Pvt Paul O. Davis, Pvt Francis A. Rocca, Pvt Raymond Smith, Pfc Frederick A. Wilhelm, Pvt John C. Ott, Pvt Jarris C. Clark, Second Lieutenant Reed Pelfrey. (NARA)

A Pathfinder draped with a battery pack that went with the "Adis" light. (NARA)

101st Pathfinders. (NARA)

101st Pathfinders. (NARA)

101st Pathfinders. (NARA)

Drop Zone: Normandy

The 502nd PIR had the worst jump pattern of all units dropped on DDay; not one of its planes found the DZ. The 501st had the best drop pattern in Normandy, as nearly all of its troops landed right on their assigned DZ. The third regiment of the division (506th PIR), was badly scattered; only nine of its planes found the DZ. Despite the bad drop and confusion, several small units within the 101st Airborne Division managed, under fiercely determined leaders, to band together and accomplish most of the division's mission before daylight.

Major General Taylor landed in a cow pasture. While still cutting himself out of his parachute harness, the general sensed that something was wrong. Nothing had looked familiar to him a few minutes before, when the pilot gave him the green jump light. But he had jumped anyhow, in the belief that his pilot could see better than he, and therefore knew where they were. Taylor was wrong. The pilot could see no better, and had given the green light a little too late.

Free from his chute now, and with his 45 in hand, Taylor began prowling through the dark, prepared to meet either friend or foe. Surprisingly, not one enemy soldier was in the neighborhood. Neither were any of the men the general had just jumped with. At just about the time he was beginning to wonder if he would ever find one of his troops, Taylor came across a lone private. Overjoyed at having found another friendly soul, the two men hugged each other.

Proceeding through the darkness, Taylor managed to gather a few more stray paratroopers, and finally started meeting members of his staff. First he met General McAuliffe, his division artillery commander, who had with him some artillerymen he had rounded up. Next he met his chief of staff, Colonel Gerald J. Higgins, and Lieutenant Colonel John Pappas, his division engineer.

Although not one planeload of Colonel Mosely's 502nd PIR was dropped into its DZ A, a good many of his troopers managed to group together and head for the regiment's primary objective: causeways 3 and 4. Colonel Mosely was unable to march with his men, for he had broken his leg upon landing. Because of his injury, Mosely was required to relinquish command of his regiment to his executive officer, Lieutenant Colonel John H. Michaelis.

Mosely had assigned the capture of causeways 3 and 4 to his 3rd Battalion commander, Lieutenant Colonel Robert G. Cole. Like so many other paratroopers that night, Cole had no idea where he was when he landed. The only thing he knew for sure was that he was not where he was supposed to be, and none of his troops were with him. After groping around awhile, Cole managed to gather up four of his men. Then he met two regimental staff officers: Major Vaughn, the S-4; and captain Buker, the S-2. After wandering around for nearly another hour with his small band, Cole came upon a house at the edge of a town and knocked on the door. A female voice speaking through the unopened door told Cole he was on the outskirts of Sainte Mére-Eglise. This news was most disheartening to Cole, for it meant that he was nearly five miles away from the vital causeways. There was nothing else to do but continue on with his mission, so Cole started marching toward the causeways. By three o'clock in the morning his band had swelled to nearly 80 troopers, only a few of whom were from his battalion.

Several of the strays were from the 82nd Airborne Division, but they tagged along anyway, feeling there was strength in numbers.

About four o'clock in the morning, Cole's force encountered a group of Germans marching toward them. A firefight erupted, during which Major Vaughn was killed and the Germans driven off. When the dust settled, Cole regrouped and continued the march toward the causeways. He arrived at causeway 4 shortly after first light, only to find it devoid of enemy troops. Leaving a small detachment, he marched one mile south to the inland end of causeway 3 where, at 7:30, he established himself without a fight.

Meanwhile, down on Utah Beach, elements of the 4th Infantry Division's 1st Battalion, 8th Infantry, which had come ashore earlier that morning, began advancing inland along causeway 3 toward Cole's men. German defenders at the shoreline offered only feeble resistance, and then retreated inland along the causeway, to what they thought was safer territory. When Coles' men saw the Germans coming they ducked down, held their fire until the last one was well inside the killing zone, and then cut loose. It was all over in less than five minutes. The Germans, all bunched up, never had a chance. Cole's men had accounted for 75 of their enemy without a single casualty among themselves.

While Cole and his men had been marching through the night toward causeways 3 and 4, Colonel Sink's 506th Parachute Infantry Regiment had been busy in the southernmost part of the huge American airhead. Sink's primary regimental mission was the capture of causeways 1 and 2. His secondary mission, almost equally important, was to seize two wooden bridges leading over the Douve River.

Sink planned to accomplish his missions by dropping into DZ C with his 1st and 2nd Battalions. To his 1st Battalion Commander, Lieutenant Colonel William L. Turner, Sink gave the relatively easy task of assembling his units after the drop and becoming the regimental reserve. To his 2nd Battalion commander, Lieutenant Colonel Robert L. Strayer, Sink assigned the regiment's primary mission. Sink's 3rd Battalion, commanded by Lieutenant Colonel Robert M. Wolwerton, had been slated to jump into DZ D. From there it was to march south and capture the two wooden bridges over the Douve.

Like nearly all other regiments that night, Sink's outfit was badly scattered on the drop. Of the two battalions that were to have been dropped in DZ C, only nine planeloads found their mark. Some two hours after the drop, Lieutenant Colonel Turner had managed to round up only 50 men of his 1st Battalion. Lieutenant Colonel Strayer's 2nd Battalion was more fortunate. It had been dropped in a fairly neat cluster, but on the wrong DZ. Strayer's men began assembling in the darkness, thinking they were on DZ C, when all the while they were three miles north of it on the edge of DZ A.

Meanwhile, on DZ D, Sink's 3rd Battalion suffered the worst fate of any battalion that jumped into Normandy. The area where this battalion was jumping into had long been recognized by the Germans as a likely spot for a parachute assault. Accordingly, they deliberately left large open fields clear of obstacles as an invitation to the Allied airborne planners. The area was ringed with numerous machine-gun emplacements, and vacant wooden barns had been soaked with oil so that, in the event of a night parachute attack,

On June 12th, the first paratroopers cross Carentan. (NARA)

they could, by the light of the blazing barns, see and kill paratroopers descending into the inferno.

By the time Sink's Battalion arrived over its DZ, the German defenders had been fully alerted and the barns were burning brightly. The German machine gunners did their job well. In a little less than 10 minutes they managed to kill the battalion commander, Lieutenant Colonel Wolverton, his executive officer, Major George Grant, and the bulk of the battalion. The only part of this unit that survived were two plane loads dropped in the wrong spot. Amazingly, these two planeloads regrouped and, under the leadership of Captain Charles Sheettle, the battalion S-3, accomplished the battalion's mission of capturing the two bridges over the Douve.

Colonel Sink himself landed without incident in a field just west of Culoville. After meeting a couple of his men he moved into the town, where he established his CP and tried, without success, to make radio contact with his three battalion commanders. At the same time, Lieutenant Colonel Strayer, the commander of the 2nd Battalion, discovered where he really was and started marching south towards his objective. Shortly after dawn, while still proceeding southward, Strayer's outfit ran into German troops. By the time Strayer managed to fight his way past the Germans and reach causeway 2, it was already in the hands of infantrymen who had come to Normandy by boat.

Due to radio difficulties, Sink knew nothing of Strayer's whereabouts, nor of his unsuccessful attempt to reach his objective before dawn. Sink therefore decided to send his reserve unit, Lieutenant Colonel Turner's 1st Battalion, to secure causeways 1 and 2. Turner's Battalion at this time consisted of about 50 men. Because his outfit was so undermanned, Sink sent it against causeway 1, the closest causeway to them. They got only partway there, however, when German machine gunners pinned them down.

While Colonel Sink's two battalions tried and failed to secure the causeways, General Taylor established his headquarters in Hiesville, right in the middle of glider LZ E. Taylor's division reserve, the 3rd Battalion, 501st PIR, commanded by Lieutenant Colonel Julian Ewell, was with him. From Hiesville, Taylor made repeated unsuccessful attempts to contact Colonel Sink by radio in order to learn whether the vital causeways had been secured. Deeply worried by his lack of communication, and fearing the worst about the causeways, Taylor dispatched his reserve-battalion commander, Ewell, and about 50 paratroopers to capture causeway 1. Shortly after eight o'clock in the morning, Ewell launched an attack against Pouppeville, a town situated on the western end of the causeway. The battle for Pouppeville dragged on until noon, at which time the German commander surrendered his troops. The cost of securing causeway one was 18 dead paratroopers.

While the battles for the causeways were in progress, Colonel Sink remained in isolation at his command post with just a handful of men. In between helping drive off German patrols trying to overrun his headquarters, the colonel tried unsuccessfully to make radio contact with his 3rd Battalion, which had jumped south into DZ D (This was the battalion that had been nearly been wiped out when it jumped into its enemy-illuminated DZ earlier that morning.). After several unanswered radio calls, Sink dispatched two foot patrols with orders to locate the 3rd Battalion. Both patrols returned, saying they could find no trace of it.

On the left, the town hall of Sainte-Marie-du-Mont, 60 years after the fighting. (D. François)

It was almost 11 o'clock in the morning, and Sink was beside himself with worry over the apparent disappearance of his 3rd Battalion. Unable to restrain himself any longer, he decided to go look for the battalion himself. Sink and his S-3, Major Hannah, mounted a jeep driven by Private George D. Rhodes, an artilleryman. For extra protection, Sink also took along two Tommy gun-carrying paratroopers, Privates Amory S. Roper and Salvadore G. Cencieros.

Driving along through the Normandy countryside, Sink's party suddenly found itself in the midst of a company of German infantry. Fortunately, the Germans were unprepared for Sink's arrival. They were reclining along the sides of the road, apparently taking a break after a long march. Upon sighting the American jeep racing past them, the Germans scrambled for cover. Meanwhile, Sink and his companions excitedly began shooting their weapons, causing everyone, including themselves, to panic. (Neither Sink, nor any of his men thought of throwing one of the many hand grenades they were carrying). Finally, Sink saw he was getting in too deep and ordered his driver to turn the jeep around and rerun the gauntlet. Miraculously, Sink made it back to his starting point without losing a man, or getting a single bullet hole in the jeep. Privates Roper and Cencieros, until they were both killed at Bastogne, frequently talked about their wild jeep ride with the colonel.

That so many paratroopers from Colonel Johnson's 501st PIR landed together in DZ D, where they were supposed to, was the result of a last-minute foul up. Just as the green light flashed on in Johnson's aircraft, a bundle that was to have been routinely pushed out the door became hung up, preventing everyone in the plane from jumping. Johnson was furious about this, but he really should have been happy, for his plane was still well short of the DZ. Some 30 seconds after the bundle was shaken loose and kicked out the door, Johnson and his troops went out right after it, to a bull's-eye landing on the correct DZ.

It was most unfortunate that on DZ D, where the drops were very accurate, the Germans were fully alerted and prepared; Colonel Johnson's 1st Battalion commander, Lieutenant Colonel Robert C. Carrol, was killed during his first few minutes in France. Carrol's executive officer, Major Philip S. Cage, was wounded and captured. Most of the 1st Battalion's staff and company commanders were missing in action for the next several days. Casualties, confusion, and Germans notwithstanding, Johnson collected a small force in the dark and captured the vital river lock at La Barquette shortly before first night.[3]

Captain Courageous: Richard Winters

Graduating from Franklin-Marshall College in June 1941 as a business major, Richard Winters volunteered for military service. His intent was to spend the mandatory one year in the Army, then return to civilian life to pursue a private career. Following his induction in August, he spent his basic combat training at Camp Croft, SC, where he was stationed when he received word of the Japanese attack on Pearl Harbor. Winters soon applied for Officer Candidate School and arrived at Fort Benning, where he graduated in July 1942 as a second lieutenant of infantry.

Seeking adventure, he next volunteered for airborne training. In Winters' eyes, the airborne training appeared to be "interesting work." The troopers were "hard, lean, bronzed, and tough... a proud and cocky bunch." Moreover, the physical training was very appealing to Winters. Standing 6 feet tall and weighing 177 pounds, he was accustomed to lots of running and outdoor activity. Also, the additional jump pay might help pay off his father's home mortgage.

When the 506th PIR was formed in August, Winters became one of the original members of Easy Company. Training at Camp Toccoa, GA, was rugged, but Winters relished the camaraderie and challenges associated with airborne training. Assigned command of Easy's 2nd Platoon, he soon completed his five jumps and received his airborne wings. In mid-April 1943 he had also assumed the duties of company executive officer, a position that he found brought new challenges. Still a first lieutenant, Winters remained with Easy Company when the regiment joined the 101st Airborne Division in June 1943. Three months later, the 506th PIR deployed to England to prepare for the ensuing invasion of the European continent.

From September 1943 until June 1944, Winters quietly emerged as Easy Company's most dynamic and charismatic junior officer. He later attributed his succes to his training, and to the relationship that he had developed with the enlisted men. As a teetotaler, he never participated in the social life associated with the officer corps. Winters preferred the life of quiet reflection and organized athletics within Easy. He described himself as a "half-breed," being an officer with the responsibility to train the men, but being an enlisted man at heart. Always weighing on his mind was the tremendous responsibility of preparing his men for combat. In a private letter home, he commented on his personal crusade to improve himself as an officer, and to improve Easy Company as fighters and as men. The net result was a highly motivated company that was poised to inflict maximum punishment on the enemy when the "big day" arrived.

For those soldiers, sailors, and airmen who participated in D-Day, June 6 was unlike any day in History. And it was on D-Day that Dick Winters had his rendezvous with destiny. Easy Company's mission, as with the other units within the 101st Airborne Division, was to seize the causeways behind Utah Beach to facilitate the expansion of the beachhead. Jumping from a C-47 Dakota at 150 miles per hour and at 500 feet and less, the Division's drop was scattered across the Cotentin Peninsula. Winters came down near the town of Ste Mere-Eglise, several kilometers from the intended drop zone. Rallying a couple of troopers, he soon was en route to Ste Marie-du-Mont, destined to be the Division's headquarters for most of D-Day. En route, Winters stumbled across the battalion staff and 40 men of D Company.

By 7:00 AM E company consisted of two light machine guns, one bazooka with no ammunition, one 60 mm mortar, nine riflemen, and two officers. No one knew the whereabouts of the company commander, so Winters took command. Three kilometers from Ste. Marie-du-Mont, the column encountered sustained enemy fire, and Winters was summoned to the front. The battalion commander informed Winters that there was a four-gun battery of German 105mm cannons a few hundred meters to the front, across an open field opposite a French farmhouse called Brécourt Manor. The battery was set up in a hedgerow, and defended by a 50-man German platoon. The guns were firing directly down a causeway leading to Utah Beach. The battalion operations officer directed Winters to take the battery. Taking his company, Winters made a careful reconnaissance and then issued orders for an assault. The attack would consist of a frontal assault led by Winters, with covering fire from several directions to pin down the Germans. Winters selected three soldiers for the assault: Pvt. Gerald Lorraine; Pvt. Popeye Wynn; and Cpl. Joe Toye. Asked later why he selected these three, Winters recalled, "In combat you look for killers." Many thought they were killers and wanted to prove it. They are, however, few and far between.

Winters saw the impending attack as a "high risk opportunity." The key was "...initiative, an immediate appraisal of situation, the use of terrain to get into the connecting trench, and taking one gun at a time." Crawling on their bellies, Winters and his men got close enough and knocked out the first gun. Mowing down the retreating Germans, Winters then placed a machine gun to fire down the trench. He had also noticed that as soon as he got close enough to assault the first gun, the Germans in an adjacent hedgerow temporary lifted their fire so that they would not inflict friendly casualties. That was enough for Winters, who had a "sixth sense" that such a respite shifted the advantage to him.

With the first gun out of action, Winters grabbed two other soldiers and charged the second gun. Throwing hand grenades and firing their rifles, they took the second howitzer. Next to the gun was a case with a map that showed all the German artillery in the Cotentin Peninsula.

Winters sent the map back to battalion headquarters, and then directed another assault that rapidly captured the third gun. Reinforcements led by an officer from D Company soon arrived. Winters briefly outlined the situation, and then watched D Company capture the last gun. With the mission complete Winters ordered a withdrawal. It was 11:30 AM, roughly three hours since Winters had received the order to take the battery. In summarizing Easy's action, historian Stephen Ambrose notes that with 12 men—what amounted to a squad—later reinforced by elements of D Company, Winters had destroyed a German battery, killed 12 Germans, wounded many more, and taken 12 prisoners. It would be a gross exaggeration to say that Easy Company saved the day at Utah Beach, but reasonable to say that it had made an important contribution to the success of the invasion. Winters' action at Brécourt Manor was a textbook infantry assault, frequently studied at the U.S Military Academy. Ever the self-effacing leader, Winters described the action to combat historian S.L.A. Marshall simply as laying down a base of fire to cover the assault. Left unsaid was his leadership by example. At every stage he had made the correct decision, from selecting the right men for each task, to making an accurate reconnaissance of the enemy position, to leading the maneuver element in person. In his own analysis, Winters credited his training and preparing for D-Day, his "apogee" in command. When the day was finally over, he wrote in his diary that if he survived the war, he would find an isolated farm somewhere and spend the rest of his life in peace. [5]

Saint Côme-du-Mont: Having arrived by glider, an officer manipulates a German rocket launcher.

Church of Saint Côme-du-Mont, 60 years after the fighting. (D.François)

In the morning of 6 June, the paratroopers meet civilians in Sainte Marie-du-Mont. (NARA)

The water pump of Sainte Marie-du-Mont today. Nothing has changed in the village. (D. François)

U.S. infantrymen discover a German-made Sd.kfz.2 *Kettenkraftad.*

Ravenoville, 6 June: Trooper Jim Flanagan of C Company of the 502nd PIR flaunts a trophy flag. (NARA)

Ravenoville, 6 June: Paratroopers of the 101st have seized a Renault caterpillar used by the enemy. (NARA)

In Sainte-Marie-du-Mont, the paratroopers of the 101st link up with the troops that have landed at Utah Beach. (NARA)

Across from the church of Saint-Côme-du-Mont, pieces of equipment abandoned by the Germans. (NARA)

The church of Saint-Côme-du-Mont today.

6 June: the paratroopers of the 101st cross Sainte-Marie-du-Mont. A few hours ago, the German General Von der Heydte was in the church steeple watching the troops land at Utah Beach. (NARA)

The village church today. (D. François)

Château de Colombières at Hiesville; it will serve as a field hospital. Many paratroopers were treated here before the bombing that destroyed the castle. Under its commander, Major Albert J. Crandall, the 326th Airborne Medical Company left Aldermaston airfield in England, at 01.19 on June 6 1944, carried by glider. The leading glider, piloted by LTC. Mike Murphy and carrying Brigadier General Don Pratt, tragically crashed. The 101st Airborne Division divisional hospital was set up at the Château de Colombières early in the morning of June 6 1944, near the divisional HQ. (NARA)

The medics remove the identification tags from the bodies before authorizing temporary burial. (Nara)

Sainte-Marie-du-Mont is liberated on 6 June. (NARA)

Sainte-Marie-du-Mont today. (D. François)

While waiting for the arrival of vehicles coming by sea, the paratroopers utilize vehicles taken from the enemy. (Nara)

These paratroopers of Signal Company distribute rations to civilian refugees at the Lecaudey farm, Headquarters of the 101st Airborne Division in Hiesville. (NARA)

General Maxwell D. Taylor, commander of the 101st Airborne Division. (NARA)

Brigadier General Anthony C. McAuliffe, Division Artillery Commander. (NARA)

For these German soldiers, the war is over. (NARA)

Utah Beach: These German prisoners wait to be transferred to England. (NARA)

A mass grave where German prisoners are laid to rest. (NARA)

A variety of weapons seized from the enemy. Among these weapons are an artillery rangefinder, a Panzerschreck and Mauser and Lebel rifles. (NARA)

MG-42 machine gun seized from the enemy. (NARA)

These infantrymen uncover a German cemetary. (NARA)

This infantryman uncovers the graves of German fighters hastily buried near a hedge, most likely on the very spot the soldiers were killed. (NARA)

A war correspondent looks for the perfect angle to photograph this soldier carrying a *Panzerscheck* killed in his own foxhole. (NARA)

Abilene Reflector-Chronicl

ONLY DAILY IN DICKINSON COUNTY ABILENE, KANSAS, TUESDAY, JUNE 6, 1944 A DICKINSON COUNTY INSTITUT

AIN FIRM GRIP ON FRENCH COA

Allied Armies Surge Into Norm
on Wide Front Under 11,000 P
as Warships Blast Nazi Coastal

Churchill Reports Invasion Going Ahead According
to Plan as Paratroopers and Glider Forces Seize Citic
and Important Communications Behind German Lines

By Associated Press

The Paris radio broadcast the report of a "Last miunte flash from the
early Tuesday evening which announced that a "vicious battle is ragi
Rouen between powerful Allied paratroop formations and German anti-in
ces." Rouen is 41 miles inland, east of Le Harve.

From the time of the first landings, a constant stream of broadcasts came
man transmitters—many of them carrying more than an indication that Hitl
along the western coast had been caught napping.

The Allied invasion armies which landed on the Normandy section of nort
early Tuesday, by evening had smashed their way inland on a broad front against
slight German opposition.

Prime Minister Churchill said that a part of the record-shattering numbe
and glider-borne troops were fighting in Cean, nine miles inland from the bay
They developed so swiftly after their silent landicating they seized a number
bridges before the Germans had a chance to demolish them. Allied supreme hea
that losses of men were much lighter than was expected. Naval losses were
"very, very light"

Enemy sources reported penetrations from two to ten miles at points
miles apart. The Allied plan seemed to include occupation of the Cherbourg

6 June: The front page of the Abilene newspaper announcing the Normandy Landings. (NARA)

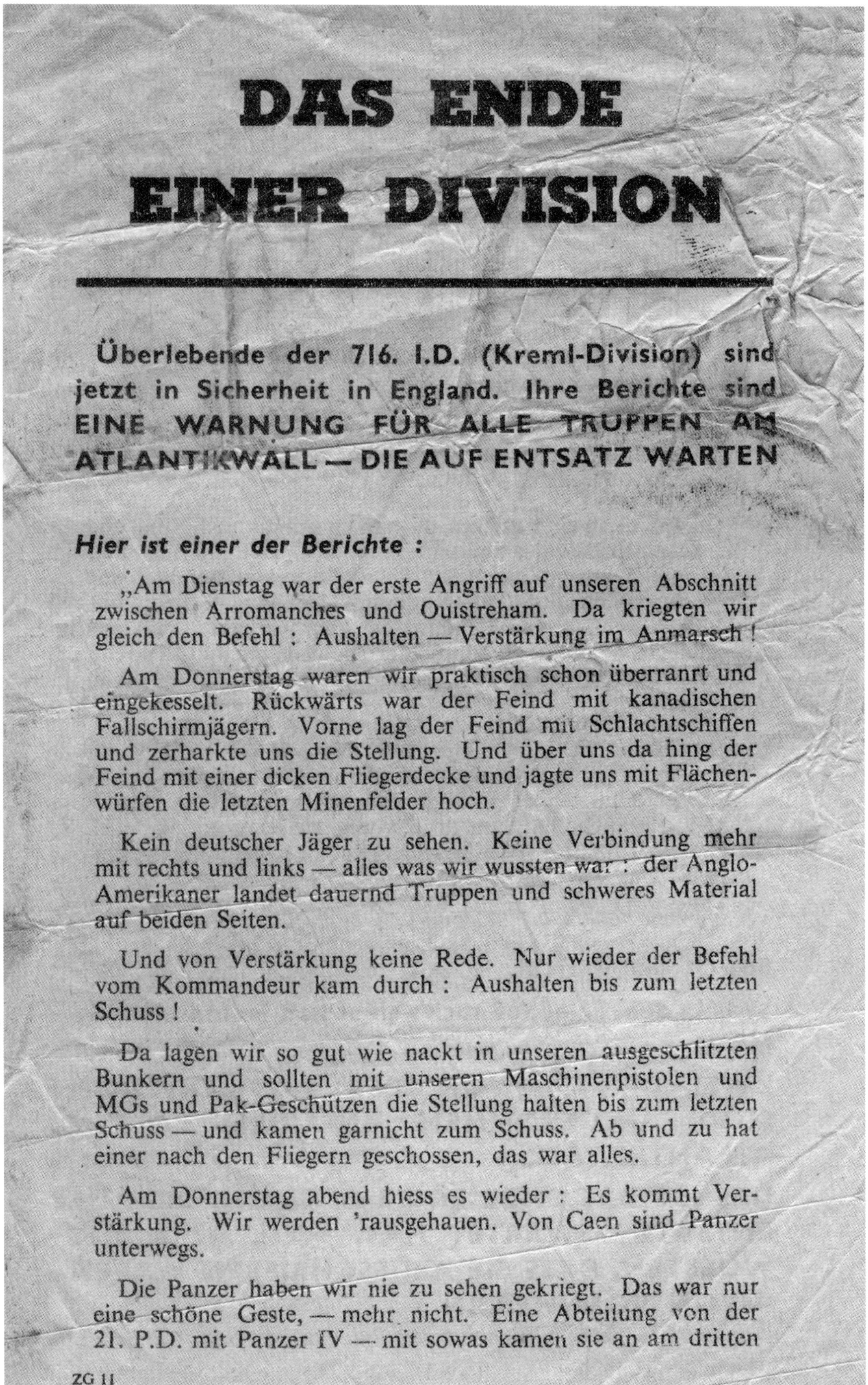

DAS ENDE EINER DIVISION

Überlebende der 716. I.D. (Kreml-Division) sind jetzt in Sicherheit in England. Ihre Berichte sind EINE WARNUNG FÜR ALLE TRUPPEN AM ATLANTIKWALL — DIE AUF ENTSATZ WARTEN

Hier ist einer der Berichte :

„Am Dienstag war der erste Angriff auf unseren Abschnitt zwischen Arromanches und Ouistreham. Da kriegten wir gleich den Befehl : Aushalten — Verstärkung im Anmarsch !

Am Donnerstag waren wir praktisch schon überrannt und eingekesselt. Rückwärts war der Feind mit kanadischen Fallschirmjägern. Vorne lag der Feind mit Schlachtschiffen und zerharkte uns die Stellung. Und über uns da hing der Feind mit einer dicken Fliegerdecke und jagte uns mit Flächenwürfen die letzten Minenfelder hoch.

Kein deutscher Jäger zu sehen. Keine Verbindung mehr mit rechts und links — alles was wir wussten war : der Anglo-Amerikaner landet dauernd Truppen und schweres Material auf beiden Seiten.

Und von Verstärkung keine Rede. Nur wieder der Befehl vom Kommandeur kam durch : Aushalten bis zum letzten Schuss !

Da lagen wir so gut wie nackt in unseren ausgeschlitzten Bunkern und sollten mit unseren Maschinenpistolen und MGs und Pak-Geschützen die Stellung halten bis zum letzten Schuss — und kamen garnicht zum Schuss. Ab und zu hat einer nach den Fliegern geschossen, das war alles.

Am Donnerstag abend hiess es wieder : Es kommt Verstärkung. Wir werden 'rausgehauen. Von Caen sind Panzer unterwegs.

Die Panzer haben wir nie zu sehen gekriegt. Das war nur eine schöne Geste, — mehr nicht. Eine Abteilung von der 21. P.D. mit Panzer IV — mit sowas kamen sie an am dritten

ZG 11

Parachuting above enemy lines in order to incite them to surrender.

The armored vehicles, having landed at Utah Beach, penetrate the Cotentin region. (Nara)

In the morning of June 6, after hard combat, this wounded German waits to be evacuated to a medical unit. (NARA)

This paratrooper inspects a piece of artillery abandoned by the enemy. (NARA)

These paratroopers, far from their drop sight, have spent several days behind enemy lines. (NARA)

German soldiers captured during the first days of fighting. They are old and unfit for combat. (NARA)

SS soldiers taken as prisoners. The Screaming Eagles will have to fight against the *Waffen SS*, the elite of the German army and against the paratroopers of General Von der Heydte. (NARA)

German paratroopers on the Normandy front. (ECPA)

German paratroopers training in Normandy. (ECPA)

German paratroopers with an MG-34 machine gun. (ECPA)

German paratroopers training in Normandy. (ECPA)

German paratroopers prepare for a drill. (ECPA)

Interesting photograph of German paratroopers and a detailed rendering of their gear. (EPCA)

German paratroopers posing with a car they have commandeered in Normandy. (EPCA)

German paratroopers setting up a machine gun. (ECPA)

A light German armored vehicle transports troops during a drill in Normandy. In a few weeks, they will be fighting against the Americans. (EPCA)

6 June 1944, Valognes: American paratroopers, taken prisoners during the night, are transferred to a prison camp. (D. François)

July 1944, Rennes, Hospital Stalag†: (left to right) Major Philip Gage (501st PIR), Seham Sigh Gyani, Major Gordon Smith (507th PIR), and Captain William Patty (A/501st PIR). (G. Smith)

Through the rubble of Carentan

Houlgate Street. (D. François)

The Barquette, today (D. François)

The Barquette, 60 years after the war. (D. François)

Memorial inaugurated to commemorate the combats of the Château de la Colombières in Hiesville, hospital of the 101st Airborne Division. (D. François)

Entrance to the Château de la Colombières (gate), destroyed in June 1944.

Interior view of the entrance to the Château de la Colombières in Hiesville.

The outbuildings of the château were damaged by the shelling.

The outbuildings today. (D. François)

Château de la Colombières after the bombing of June 9th.

After the bombing, the château was gutted out. On the second floor, one notices the beautiful XVIth Century fireplace.

Ravaged by the bombing, the château will unfortunately be reduced to rubble.

Plaque placed at the entrance to Lecaudey Farm recalling the presence here of the 101st Airborne Division HQ. (D. François)

Major General Taylor at the wheel of his jeep in the farmyard. (NARA)

The Lecaudey farm today. (D. François)

At the end of the war, German prisoners wait to be evacuated to Utah Beach and then on to England. (NARA)

Aerial view of the Bocage Normand†: Many gliders landed in the small pastures of the Cotentin.

Silent wings

On the night of 6 June, the assistant division commander, Brigadier General Don F. Pratt, led 52 gliders during the invasion. Although all of the pilots managed to put down within two miles, only six of them landed in the designated zone. Intelligence reports had not mentioned that most fields were bordered with hedgerows, four-foot earthen fences covered with a tangle of hedges, bushes, and trees. Due to the darkness and the hazard caused by these hedgerows, five soldiers were killed in landing. One of them was Brigadier General Pratt.

Glider elements of the 101st played only minor roles on D-Day. Before dawn, two batteries of the 81st Airborne AAA/AT Battalion plus staff, engineer, signal, and medical elements—amounting to 155 personnel, 25 jeeps, one midget bulldozer, and 16 pounder guns—took off in 52 Wacos. One, carrying the Division headquarters' radion set, parted tow near the departure field; the signalmen hurriedly headed back to the airfield, hired another aircraft, and joined a later airlift. Despite an orderly Pathfinder reception, mishaps cut arrivals on or near LZ "E" to just 21 gliders, shortly after 0400 hours. Ten more alit nearly two miles away at Les Forges, and the remaining 18 were everywhere and nowhere; due to the dark, crisscross hedgerows, tall trees, and uneven ground, most gliders were rendered hors d'combat on landing.

Reinforcements arrive by glider at the la Londe airfield in the area of Sainte Mère Eglise. (NARA)

6 June, 1944, a British-made glider, Horsa, has overturned while attempting to land in the area of Sebeville. Its occupants were killed from the shock. (NARA)

Horsa glider: the men are busy unloading a jeep. (NARA)

A Waco glider has landed safely in a field in Normandy. The cows seem puzzled at the presence of such an unfamiliar object. (NARA)

A Waco glider has crashed into a hedgerow in the Bocage Normand region. (NARA)

This gliderman has not survived the crash of his glider. The prospect of losses for troops coming by glider was much greater than those dropped from the air by parachutes. (NARA)

6 June at dawn: one of the first victims, probabaly killed a few minutes after landing his Waco. (NARA)

Text of the Memorial of General Pratt in Hiesville. (D. François)

Memorial for General Pratt erected at the angle of the field where his glider crashed on 6 June 1944. (D. François)

Photo showing the crash of General Pratt's glider in Hiesville.

Carentan

From its initial D-Day objectives, the 101st Airborne Division was ordered to push south and size the city of Carentan. There it was to effect a juncture with the V Corps, which had landed on Omaha Beach. Carentan fell after a violent three-day battle, during which the Screaming Eagles suffered heavily, but wiped out the German 6th Parachute Regiment.

On its way south to Carentan, Lieutenant Colonel Cole's 3rd Battalion 502nd PIR advanced to within a few miles of the city limits, where it ran into determined resistance at a site known as Bridge 4. Heavy small-arms fire coming from a farmhouse about 300 yards off to the right of the bridge was chopping Cole's battalion to pieces. He tried bombarding the farmhouse with artillery, but even that failed to diminish enemy fire. This left Cole with two possible courses of action. He could stay put until heavy, direct-fire weapons could be brought up from the rear. Or, he could make a bold frontal attack in an attempt to overrun the farmhouse. To stay put would mean additional casualties and the loss of forward motion. Cole decided to attack.

Cole yelled across the road to his executive officer, Major John P. Stopka: *"Tell everyone to fix bayonets. When I blow my whistle, I want everyone to charge that farmhouse."*

Pausing only long enough for his order to get passed and the artillery to shift from high explosive to smoke rounds, Cole gave a loud blast on his whistle and started running straight for the farmhouse. After he had advanced about 50 yards, he looked back to see how well his battalion was doing. What he saw stunned him. Only 20 men were following him. Far off to his left, Cole saw Major Stopka dashing forward, shooting his pistol, with only another 50 or so men following.

Cole's battalion had not deserted him. The reason so few men were participating in the charge was that Cole's vital fix-bayonets-and-charge-on-the-whistle order failed to reach all of the men in his battalion. As the order was being passed from man to man German mortar fire was raining down, killing troopers all along the line. And as the troopers got killed, the message they were to pass along died with them.

Cole and Stopka were more than halfway to the objective when the remainder of the battalion caught sight of them. Several small groups of paratroopers tried to catch up with them, but were unable to do so because of their late start. Amazingly, the small bayonet charge carried the objective. Cole received the Congressional Medal of Honor for leading it, but he never got to wear it; a sniper killed him three months later in Holland. For his part in the charge, Stopka got a Distinguished Service Cross pinned on him two weeks before he was killed at Bastogne.

Carentan fell to the 101st Airborne Division on June 12. Shortly thereafter, the division had to fight hard against a heavy German counterattack (that employed tanks, artillery, SS troops, and paratroopers fighting as infantry) to keep it. With considerable assistance from the Air Corps and the 2nd Armored Division, Taylor's paratroopers and glidermen were able to beat off the Germans and retain their grip on the town. Except for a few small, limited objective attacks made a few days later, the battle for Carentan marked the end of the Normandy fighting for the 101st Airborne.[4]

Post card of Carentan at the beginning of the Century.. (Coll. Marcel Corbet)

Post card of the Place de la République. (Coll. Marcel Corbet)

Post card of the Canal de Carentan, before the war. (Coll. Marcel Corbet)

Overall view of Carentan before he war. (Coll. Marcel Corbet)

The train station of Carentan. (Coll. Marcel Corbet)

At the end of the Battle of Carentan, General Taylor congratulates the men of the 101st Airborne during a ceremony at the Place de la République. (NARA)

The Arcades, Place de la République in Carentan. (D. François)

At the end of the Battle of Carentan, civilians cheer the paratroopers of the 101st on. (NARA)

The first jeeps brought by gliders cross Carentan. (NARA)

The paratroopers of the 101st Airborne cross Carentan after heavy fighting with the paratroopers of Von der Heydte. (NARA)

After heavy fighting, the houses of Carentan are in flames. (NARA)

Infantrymen of the 101st Airborne looking at a destroyed house in the area of Carentan. (NARA)

14 June, 1944, Carentan: A paratrooper of the 101st Airborne has appropriated a *Kettenkraftrad*, probably seized from the paratroopers of the 6 *Fallschirmjager* Regiment. (NARA)

13 June, on the road to Périers, near Carentan, the paratroopers have set up a 57mm artillery canon. (NARA)

West of Carentan, the Cherbourg-Paris railroad track was destroyed by the German paratroopers. (NARA)

A U.S. medic treats an SS of the *Waffenn SS 17th Panzergrenadier Division*. (NARA)

The paratroopers of the 502nd PIR have seized an enemy *Kettenkraftrad* that will be highly prized by the American airborne troops. (NARA)

Civilians from Carentan place flowers on the makeshift tomb of a paratrooper. (NARA)

A soldier who has most likely arrived by glider takes a break with a child from Carentan. (NARA)

A few hours after the Battle of Carentan, civilians begin to emerge out of their shelters in order to meet the paratroopers of the 101st Airborne on the Place de la République. (NARA)

Memorial for the dead, Place de la République in Carentan. (D. François)

20 June: A ceremony is organized on the Place de la République by the liberators of Carentan to honor the paratroopers of the 101st Airborne Division. (NARA)

An American doctor has just delivered a child in Carentan. This is the first child born after the liberation of the town. (NARA)

In the church of Carentan, a prayer service is organized for the liberators of the town. (NARA)

A church is hit by artillery fire in the area of Carentan. (NARA)

A few weeks after the liberation of Carentan, a ceremony is organized by civilian authorities at the memorial for the dead. English soldiers are invited to represent Great Britain. (NARA)

12 June: Paratroopers of the 501st PIR advance slowly in the streets of Carentan. Enemy snipers slow down their progress. (NARA)

18 June, 1944: Armoured vehicles that have landed at Utah Beach arrive at Carentan. (NARA)

The railroad tracks in Carentan, 60 years after the war. (D. François)

A soldier of the 327th GIR in the center of Carentan. In the foreground, civilians appear to relax after the fighting. (NARA)

The main square of Carentan, today. (D. François)

An armoured enemy vehicle destroyed in Carentan. (NARA)

An artillery barrage is carried out in order to dislodge the enemy that is solidly entrenched around Carentan. (NARA)

Aerial view of Carentan. (NARA)

In the neighboring villages, civilians acclaim the liberators and place flags on the memorials for the dead. (NARA)

12 June: After deadly combats, the paratroopers of the 101st Airborne enter Carentan. (NARA)

Houlgate Street, Carentan. (D. François)

Carentan, 12 June 1944: Glidermen and paratroopers watch the passing parade. A jeep, and a gun of the 81st Airborne AAA Battalion. (NARA)

Aerial view of Carentan after the bombings. 270 houses were destroyed and 50 civilians killed. (NARA)

12 June: The "Screaming Eagles" have just taken Carentan. The town will remain under enemy fire until 20 June. (NARA)

Houlgate Street, today in Carentan. (D. François)

Aerial view of Carentan: The Fifteenth Century church was not damaged by the shelling. (NARA)

The people of the County of Manche at war.

Having established a solid bridgehead, the Americans now aimed to head up Cotentin and take Cherbourg, and maybe send troops southwards at the same time. But in view of the German resistance, this plan had to be significantly scaled down. Whether liberated or not, the people of Manche were in for a terrifying baptism of fire.

June 7th 1944

What was the situation in the Cotentin peninsula? For the Allies, there was good news and bad news. There was no denying that the landing on Utah beach had been one of the previous day's most dazzling successes, with light casualties, a rapid advance inland, the linkup with the 101st Airborne, and a solid hold on Sainte-Mere-Eglise.

For those who had arrived by air, matters were much more variable: scattered over an area 50 km long (from Graignes to Saint-Vaast), the paratroopers had not achieved all their objectives (in particular, crossing the marshes between Sainte-Mere-Eglise and Picauville), and had suffered heavy casualties. But overall, the Americans could consider the result of their first day of fighting in the Cotentin positive.

They now had to drive home their advantage, storm the Germans, and march on Cherbourg as soon as possible. In the Allies' plan, the great port was to be captured by D-Day plus 8 (June 14th), leaving one week for this achievement. And to the south, the Americans reckoned it would take between 17 and 20 days to reach Granville and Avranches.

But after a few days, the Americans had to admit that meeting the deadlines would be difficult. They no longer had the secret weapon that had helped them so much on June 6th—the surprise factor. The Germans had speedily recovered from the shock of the invasion, and General Collins' VIIth Army Corps were meeting with fierce resistance.

To the south, there was a stalemate situation at Carentan, which was only liberated on June 12th after the final bayonet attack by the 101st Airborne. But once that was done, the Germans, in firm control of the roads to Périers and Saint-LÙ, then kept the American troops at the same spot for nearly a month without letting them advance an inch.

That put the schedule back to Granville by D-Day +17, and Avranches by D-Day + 20. Things were no better to the north. It took the 4th Division infantrymen five days of hard combat before they finally silenced the batteries at Crisbecq and Azeville. On June 14th they reached Quinéville...but Montebourg was still in German hands, and all American attacks had been repelled since June 8th.

So what about the west? The Americans finally crossed the Fiére (Merderet River) after three days of butchery. The way was clear for passage to the west coast. But the 90th Infantry Division, which took over from the 82nd Airborne, was traumatised by its baptism of fire, and three days passed before its men made any real progress.

This was bad news for the Americans, who were late for their appointment at Cherbourg. Rather then getting tangled up in Montebourg, Bradley decided to change plans and strike out west to seal off the peninsula. The 82nd Airborne Division, once again at the head of the assault, took Saint-Sauveur-le-Vicomte on June 16th, while the 9th Division sped towards Barneville-Carteret, which was liberated in the morning on June 18th. This maneuver succeeded, opening up a wider theatre for Collins' army, previously hemmed in by the limited area conquered so far with varying degrees of difficulty. The Americans could now settle in more comfortably, set up airfields, store their equipment, and park the vehicles that were still arriving via Utah Beach. They had also trapped some 40,000 German soldiers in the north of the peninsula.

But Collins' men had no time to rest. From June 19th-22nd a terrible three-day storm damaged the artificial "mulberry" harbors in Calvados. Capturing Cherbourg without delay now became the most urgent Allied objective, as the Americans were in danger of being cut off from their supplies while Arromanche harbor was being repaired.

Spreading his three infantry divisions across the whole breadth of the peninsula (the 9th to the west, the 79th in the centre, and the 4th to the east), Collins had his men steamroll ahead. The steamroller went all the faster, as the Germans had withdrawn to Fortress Cherbourg: Montebourg, Bricquebec and Les Pieux fell on June 19th; and Valognes, Quettehou, and Saint-Pierre-Eglise were liberated on the 20th. On June 21st, the American vanguard finally made contact with the first defense lines of the "Festung von Cherbourg."

Notes:

1 The 101st Airborne Division WWII Website: www.ww2-airborne.us/18corps/101abn/101_overview.html

2 The 101st Airborne Division WWII Website: www.ww2-airborne.us/18corps/101abn/101_overview.html

3 Gerard M. Devlin, *Paratrooper!* (St. Martin's Press. New York)

4 Gerard M. Devlin, *Paratrooper!* (St. Martin's Press. New York)

5 Colonel Cole C. Kingseed: Major Winters Website

Epilogue

D-DAY + 33

On June 27th, D-Day plus 21, three American infantry divisions captured Cherbourg, the Neptune objective.

The capture of one of Europe's finest commercial ports had exacted a heavy toll in American lives: Battle casualties sustained by Lightning Joe Collins' VII Corps since D-Day totaled 22,119, including 2,811 killed, 13,564 wounded, and 5,665 missing (most captured, many drowned). Best estimates available for German losses in the Cherbourg campaign were 47,000 killed, wounded, or captured, including six generals.

The 82nd and 101st Airborne Divisions suffered particularly—their losses included 41 percent of VII Corps' total casualties. The All-American sustained 4,480 men killed, wounded, missing, or captured, and the Screaming Eagles had an almost identical total—4,670 casualties. In addition, during the airborne assault in the early hours of D-Day, 60 percent of supplies and heavy equipment dropped by parachute or landed by glider were destroyed, damaged, or missing.

After 33 days of continuous fighting, the 101st Airborne was relieved and allowed to return to England for further training. Elements of the Division received the Distinguished Unit Citation, and the division commander earned the Distinguished Service Cross.

Throughout the rest of the summer the Allied airborne forces prepared for several major operations, all of which were cancelled because of the speed of the Allied advance. Logistical problems and stiffening German resistance slowed the Allies short of the German border. On 17 September, the 101st took part in the largest and most daring airborne operation of the war, Operation MARKET GARDEN.

Returning to England, the first casualties of the 101st Airborne land in Southampton. This wounded soldier is an officer of the 506th PIR. (NARA)

The wounded from the Normandy combats get to England on LSTs. (NARA)

A church service is organized in the makeshift cemetery of Carentan to honor those who have fallen on the field of honor. (NARA)

Returning from Normandy, the paratroopers of the 101st Airborne land in Southampton. (NARA)

Under the watchful eye of a partrooper of the 101st, German prisoners dig graves for the paratroopers fallen in combat. (NARA)

Upon their return to England, the wounded are led to English hospitals. (NARA)

These two glidermen who have returned to England have kept some mementos from the Battle of Normandy: a Walther P-38 and a Schmeisser MP-40. (NARA)

Occupation currency brought by the Allies to Normandy.

A 100 franc bill signed by a division of paratroopers in remembrance of time spent in Normandy.

Billboard commemorating the role the 101st Airborne Division played in the Cotentin. (D. François)

A French girl places flowers over the freshly dug grave of an American glider soldier killed during the D-Day invasion. (NARA)

Appendix

Unit Commanders

Divisional HQ:
Commander: Major-General Maxwell Taylor
Chief of Staff: Colonel Gerald Higgins
Division Artillery Commander: Brigadier-General Anthony C. McAuliffe

501st Parachute Infantry Regiment:
Commander:
Lieutenant-Colonel Howard Johnson
1st Battalion:
Commander: Lieutenant-Colonel Harry Kinnard
2nd Battalion:
Commander: Major Robert Ballard
3rd Battalion:
Commander: Major Julian Ewell

502nd Parachute Infantry Regiment
Commander: Colonel George V.H. Moseley
1st Battalion:
Commander: Lieutenant-Colonel Patrick Cassidy
2nd Battalion:
Commander: Lieutenant-Colonel Elbridge Chapman
3rd Battalion:
Commander: Lieutenant-Colonel Robert Cole

506th Parachute Infantry Regiment
Commander: Colonel Robert F. Sink
1st Battalion:
Commander: Lieutenant-Colonel James Laprade
2nd Battalion:
Commander: Lieutenant-Colonel Robert Strayer
3rd Battalion:
Commander: Major Oliver Horton

327th Glider Infantry Regiment
Commander: Colonel Joseph P. Harper
1st Battalion:
Commander: Lieutenant-Colonel Hartford Sallee
2nd Battalion:
Commander: Lieutenant-Colonel Thomas Rouzie
1st Battalion 401st Glider Infantry Regiment:
Commander: Lieutenant-Colonel Roy Allen

Divisional Artillery:
Commander: Brigadier-General Anthony McAuliffe

377th Parachute Field Artillery Battalion:
Commander: Lieutenant-Colonel Harry Elkins

321st Glider Field Artillery Battalion:
Commander: Lieutenant-Colonel Edward Carmichaél

907th Glider Field Artillery Battalion:
Commander: Colonel Clarence Nelson

81st Anti-Tank Battalion:
Commander: Lieutenant-Colonel X. Cox

Divisional units:
326th Airborne Engineer Battalion
Commander: Lieutenant-Colonel John Pappas

326th Airborne Medical Company
Commander: Major William Barfield

426th Airborne Quartermasters Company

Signals Company

Reconnaissance Platoon

Military Police

Helmet of the Company HQ du 501st PIR. (Coll. B. Foucher)

Helmet of the 501st PIR, found in Saint-Côme-du-Mont. (Coll. B. Foucher)

M2 helmet of Corporal Michael A.Grodack, Company A, found in Saint-Martin-de-Varreville. (Coll. B.Foucher)

Helmet of Capitaine Twohig, 502nd PIR, Company HQ. (Coll. B. Foucher)

Helmet of the 502nd PIR, Company HQ. (Coll. B. Foucher)

M1 helmet of Lieutenant Joseph Pangerl, 502nd PIR, Company HQ. (Coll.B.≤ Foucher)

Paratrooper liner of the 506th PIR, 1st Bn, found in Saint-Côme-du-Mont. (Coll.B. Foucher)

Camouflage M2 helmet of the 502nd PIR. (Coll.B. Foucher)

M2 helmet of the 506th PIR 1st Bn, from Saint-Côme-du-Mont. (Coll.B. Foucher)

M2 helmet of the 506th PIR, 3rd Bn, du Sergant Clever, G Company. (Coll.B. Foucher)

Camouflage M-1 helmet of the 506th PIR, 3rd Bn, found in Brucheville. (Coll.B. Foucher)

Liner of Private Albert R. Jaeger, 401st GIR (3rd Bn/327th GIR) killed on June 11th 1944. (Coll.B. Foucher)

Helmet of the 327th GIR, 2nd Bn, found in Carentan. (Coll.B. Foucher)

Helmet of the 327th GIR, HQ Company. (Coll. B. Foucher)

Helmet of the 327th GIR, 1st Bn. (Coll.B. Foucher)

Helmet of the 506th PIR, HQ Company. (Coll.B. Foucher)

Helmet of the 326th AEB, found in Angoville. (Coll. B. Foucher)

Helmet of the 326th AEB. (Coll. B. Foucher)

Helmet of the 326th AEB, 2nd Company. (Coll. B. Foucher)

Helmet of the Headquarters Divisional Artillery Battalion. (Coll. B. Foucher)

Helmet of the 377th PFAB, found in Vierville. (Coll. B. Foucher)

Medic helmet.(Coll. B. Foucher)

Helmet of the101st Division HQ Company. (Coll. B. Foucher)

Helmet of the 801st Airborne Ord. Company. (Coll. B. Foucher)

Liner of the 801st Airborne Ord. Company. (Coll. B. Foucher)

Helmet of the MP Divisional 101st Airborne, having belonged to Caporal John R. Connoly. (Coll. B. Foucher)

Helmet of the 81st Airborne Antitank and Antiaircraft Bn. (Coll. B. Foucher)

Helmet of the 326th Airborne Medical Company, S/Sgt Melvin Franck. (Coll. B. Foucher)

Radio bag marked with the invasion code marked F.L (Pathfinder de la 101st)

Camouflage musette bag of Captain Harry Larson, 502nd PIR C Company. (Coll. B. Foucher)

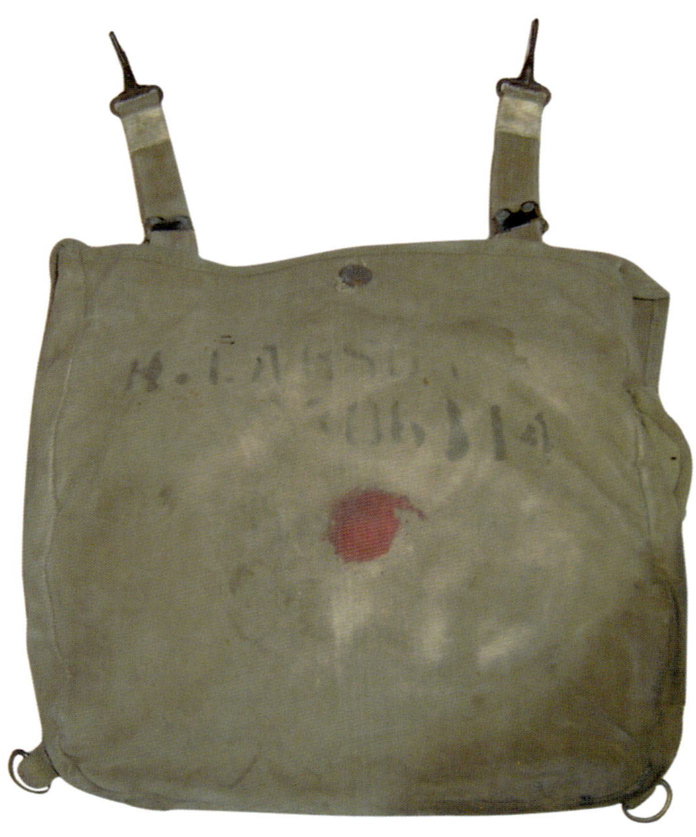

M-1942 Jump jacket of Major William Leach HQ Co, 506th PIR. (Coll. B. Foucher)

Jump jacket with pockets added on of 1st Lieutenant George Lavenson, E CO, 506th PIR. It is the only jacket known to have eight pockets. (Coll. B. Foucher)

Mae West of the 502nd PIR marked GVM (George V. Moseley) (Coll. B. Foucher)

Mae West of the 506th PIR marked RS (Robert Sink). (Coll. B. Foucher)

Mae West of the 501st PIR marked G with zipper (Geronimo†: battle cry of the 501st). (Coll. B. Foucher)

Bibliography

Gerard M. Devlin, *Paratrooper!* (St Martin's Press, New York)

John Heegan, *Six Armies in Normandy* (A Penduin Book, New York)

Stephen E. Ambrose, *D-Day, June 6, 1944: the climate battle of World War II* (Simon & Schuster, New York)

USA Airborne, 60th Anniversary (Turner Publishing, Paducah KY)

S.L.A Marshall, *Night Drop* (The Battery Press, Inc, Nasville TE)

Gen. James M. Gavin, *On to Berlin* (Bantam book)

Scrapbook, 506th Parachute Infantry Regiment (20 July 1942-4 July 1945)

The Epic of the 101st Airborne 1945